DIVORCING
INTO
Paradise

Seeing The Truth About Love

JENNIFER KING

DIVORCING INTO PARADISE
Seeing The Truth About Love
Jennifer King

Copyright © July 2024 by Jennifer King

All rights reserved. No part of this publication may be reproduced, distributed, or transmitted in any form or by any means, including photocopying, recording, or other electronic or mechanical methods, without the prior written permission of the publisher, except in the case of brief quotations embodied in critical reviews and certain other noncommercial uses permitted by copyright law.

For permission requests, write to the publisher, addressed "Attention: Permissions Coordinator," at adminservices@pecantreebooks.com

ISBN: 979-8-9913711-0-0 (Paperback)
ISBN: 979-8-9913711-1-7 (Digital)
Library of Congress Control Number: 2024919155

Interior and Cover Design by Charlyn Strachan

Pecan Tree Publishing
Hollywood, FL 33020
www.pecantreebooks.com

Conceptualizing, Creating, and Curating
Powerful Words Before and Beyond the Book
www.pecantreebooks.com
@pecantreepub – on all social media
Hollywood, FL

DEDICATION

Thank you, JC, for being one of the best parts of my life. I owe you a debt of gratitude. This book is dedicated to you, Clarence Andre King Jr AKA JC.

It took me more than a decade to write it after I initially pitched the idea to you. You thought it was a great idea, and I am glad I could finally do this – for both of us.

ADVANCE PRAISE FOR
DIVORCING INTO PARADISE

Above all, the book is candid, cathartic, enticing, and a very easy read that feeds the soul.

> Dr. Bonnie W. Salahuddin,
> Clinical Psychologist (RET).

At first read, I could not put it down. It's unique. It brought back memories of the life between myself, my daughter, and my father. I can do things better.

> Garry Baxter,
> Educator; Grimsby, England

This author paints a beautiful portrait of love as patience, longsuffering, and forgiveness. The book is inspiring and life altering! It is a «must read».

> Patricia Rembert,
> M.S.ED, M.ED-EDL,
> NASA Mathematician, Life Coach

CONTENTS

Dedication.. v
Advance Praise for *Divorcing Into Paradise*.............vii
Introduction xi

Chapter 1:   Reality Hits 15
Chapter 2:   Turbulent Childhood........................... 20
Chapter 3:   Slackened to be Awakened................ 26
Chapter 4:   New Awakenings 33
Chapter 5:   Leaving Home 44
Chapter 6:   Transitioning 47
Chapter 7:   Our New Beginning 53
Chapter 8:   Unfulfillment.. 62
Chapter 9:   Moving On 66
Chapter 10:   Re-directed..81
Chapter 11:   Additions to Our Family...................... 90
Chapter 12:   Marching Onward................................ 96

Chapter 13:	Set Back	102
Chapter 14:	Lived Experiences	105
Chapter 15:	The Uncovering	117
Chapter 16:	Easing into friendship	121
Chapter 17:	Connected at The Hip	127
Chapter 18:	Time for travel	129
Chapter 19:	Crossroads	137
Chapter 20:	Alzheimer's Observed	146
Chapter 21:	Back on the scene	154
Chapter 22:	Re-connecting as friends	160
Chapter 23:	Boyfriend Drama	163
Chapter 24:	Everything Must Change	176
Chapter 25:	The End of an Era	184

INTRODUCTION

If you picked up this book, then you certainly have been in love at least once in your lifetime. I'm not talking about the kind of love you feel toward a child, a parent, or even a friend. I am talking about that kind of love you feel for a person you engage romantically.

When you are in love, there is an unknown sensation that bears no comparison to anything you have ever felt. It feels warm, light, giddy, fuzzy, restless, a bit confusing; and there is a sense of fascination with this person. The energy is palpable.

As the first touch or kiss sends you into the stratosphere, you ask yourself, "Wow what was that? What are these feelings in my tummy that feel like butterflies?" There is nothing as good as falling in love when you least expect it.

You want to be with this person every waking hour. You think about them all of the time and make every attempt to be together as often as possible.

You can spend an insurmountable amount of time talking on the phone, neither one willing to be the 1st to hang up. You dream about the things you have already done and the many more things you now want to do with them. Occasionally you drift in and out of reality and daydream about how you can't live without them. You know this is the one for you.

You may have been in love before with other people, but you have never felt this kind of love, which makes you smile even when you're simply thinking of them. The feelings are magical. You feel passion and eroticism. You marvel at how much you need this person in your life. Am I right?

You've more than likely experienced storge love, where you deeply love your parents or your children. There is also agape love, which is the highest form of love, charity, and the love of God. Agape love is to be spread in all circumstances. Then there's philia love which is a fondness or friendship for someone.

But now you are experiencing eros love. This love is erotic and takes you into unchartered waters. You feel deep passion, sexual desire, and lust, you go all out to fully experience these new feelings. It feels good, it feels right. You start to take stock of who you are and how you can place this other person in your life.

Perhaps other love relationships developed out of loneliness, trauma, fear, and a deep desire for a fuller feeling experience. But now you feel a wanting of togetherness, presence, better sex, adventure, and family ties. From there you start to see a future based on the landscape before you. If there are children or other loved ones involved, you start to visualize having a blended family and if not, you consider how soon you can start a family.

There is a lot of mental and emotional work going on here. You may wonder how you got there. You may question yourself. Am I good enough for this person? Is this the right one for me, or am I passing through some fleeting phase? These questions sometimes go on for a year or two before marriage or sometimes of the moment you start dating. That eros love is like a bug bite or a drug that has delivered a powerful high that feels unbelievably good.

At some point there is inner dialogue. Doubt and fear from past hurts and letdowns from other relationships crop up. You wonder if this new relationship would be good for your life. Perhaps you've been culturized in this manner. There are some who may seek the advice of parents, friends, clergy, a therapist, while most simply go for it.

As you start to ponder living the rest of your life with this person, you go forth and have no second thoughts. You are ready for commitment and or marriage. You feel as though you could not live without them. Unfortunately, there is possibly little to no talk of finances, credit, bank accounts or careers. You just rush in and do it before it all goes away.

CHAPTER 1

Reality Hits

You planned your wedding, said your vows, celebrated with friends and loved ones, went on your honeymoon and now reality kicks in. You begin to experience the attitudes and habits of your new partner. Some of them are livable and some are beginning to make you crazy. But you are married now and need to work through these thoughts and feelings. Most of us say I will change him or her, or I will just learn to live with it.

You may start to shift your single life habits. You begin to have fewer conversations with close friends and family. You may begin to alienate yourself from the social things you used to do. You begin to do everything in your life as a couple, even dressing alike. Two become one and marriage takes place.

Now you have hunkered down and begin noticing the behavior of your spouse. There may be immediate vying for who will be the boss in the relationship, creating competition within the marriage. You may start to feel as though this marriage is not like what you thought it would be. There may be thoughts of self-doubt and fear of speaking up about the feelings that are erupting. You don't know how to communicate these feelings. You begin to think, "They might not want me anymore if I bring up some of these concerns." It seemed easy enough to stay quiet.

This competition for power goes on with unspoken decisions as to who is most powerful. Who is the most controlling? In other words, in this eros love relationship, who is the drug addict and who is the drug pusher? The one who has the most love is the drug pusher and the one who needs the love is the drug addict.

Within the first year of marriage, you have your first child, and now they become the object of your love. You love your spouse, but the baby needs more attention. Your spouse starts to feel rejected as you deny affection and sex. There is no conversation about feelings of post-partum blues or why the desire for sex has waned. The stress of the first year of marriage seems even more daunting. This can be the slippery slope that turns your marriage around.

There might be inner dialogue noting that the relationship is not going as planned (if you had taken time to plan it). The inner talk continues: "What should you say? To whom can you talk? Some might judge me. I told you so. Did you think this whole thing through? Should we have dated a little longer, so I could have considered what might happen later?" The inner chatter is painful and self-loathing.

Decisions must be made as to who will be the bread winner and often times it's the man, with the wife staying at home to keep the children. This creates more stress in the marriage and meanwhile no one is having a conversation about what is going on. The band just plays on. The man starts to feel a bit left out, because the attention is now going to the children and there is less attention given to him, especially sexual attention. Women on the other hand operate in a feeling nature, and sometime find sex less interesting when taking care of young children. The task of caring for a newborn and worrying if the baby is okay is filled with fear. The long hours of the day are often followed by sleepless nights as the baby doesn't know night from day. They just cry often while you have to decipher if they're wet, hungry, or uncomfortable. Chores are often done while trying to pamper the baby, including preparing dinner and cleaning up. And finally, there is sheer exhaustion.

The wife starts to feel that her husband is not helping with household duties, and she starts to feel less than appreciated. The husband is also feeling the same way, but neither one is able to talk about it. Yet, in their minds, something does not feel right. Happiness is waning.

There is even fear of not knowing how to communicate these feelings. Here the erosion of the marriage begins. You are now married, have children and financial responsibilities, but who told you that you both have a responsibility to yourselves first and then to each other? No one.

Each one of us is here on Earth with our own set of desires, wants, needs, and expectations. We have been brainwashed into thinking that all of those things come to us solely from someone else, in this case our perspective spouse, but that is not the truth. We have within, a self-awareness of how our lives should be, but we are fearful of being alone, or so we think we are alone. We are fearful to even think about our options because we know what we have now, but don't know what the future holds. It's as though '*something*' within is saying, you are unhappy and should do something about it.

We ignore this '*something*' and turn away blindly in fear. Fear of the unknown. We find it hard to work through our own problems without opening the trunks of our past lives and dumping on the marriage. We don't know how to honor the fact that we both had lives before any of this, and those lives still lie within us as shadows, waiting to be attended.

CHAPTER 2

Turbulent Childhood

I grew up in two turbulent households. My parents got divorced when I was six years old, and my brother was three. My mother later remarried when I was 10 years old, and my brother was seven. Our stepfather was nice - at times - but could be extremely violent when he was drinking. He and my mother were sociable and had a group of friends with whom they had monthly rotating house parties. My mother annexed a family room to our home. They bought a pool table and worked on weekends building a bar to sit 10 people. They prepared for their quarterly parties.

What was most perplexing about my stepfather, is the level of violence he inflicted on our family. Whenever they went out to a party, they would come home drunk and fight. He had a sawed-off shotgun that he kept in the hallway closet, wrapped inside an old military jacket. He threatened to shoot my mother, brother, and I with it on numerous occasions.

Once he grabbed her by the face and tried to bite her eye out. She had tooth marks over her eyebrow and under her eye, which became swollen, puffy, and discolored. She was kicking and screaming, and my brother and I were punching him. Blood came streaming down her face. She ran into her bathroom, yelling for us to go back to bed. This frightened me to death. I didn't know what to do with this feeling, I cried myself to sleep.

Four years of this abuse took a toll on my brother and me. One day, with the help of our childhood friend and neighbor, we decided to hatch a plan to kill him. My neighbor, Joe, had handguns, shot guns and hunting knives of all sizes. We lived on a canal and the three of us would often spend time together there to see what we could catch. He taught us how to fish as well as net fish near the surface. He showed us how to catch snails, and clean, cook and eat them. He loved the outdoors and had an army of frogs and rabbits in his bedroom. He also had a small green snake, which he kept in a fish tank with a lid.

My brother and I often spoke to Joe about the terror we felt every time our stepfather hit our mother. Joe said he and his family were aware of the abuse. I asked him to teach me how to fire one of his shot guns; and he agreed. In a couple of tries, I felt knowledgeable enough to shoot it, and so did my brother. We practiced how to cock the gun, put in the bullet shells, and close it back. We practiced shooting the shotgun into the canal.

My brother and I decided we would carry out our revenge on a Friday night, because that's when they would go out to party. We knew without a doubt that we would be awakened by her screams and his yelling and furniture being thrown around their bedroom. We would usually cry and agonize because we felt helpless to do anything about it. We had such hatred for him.

One Friday night, we were awakened in time to see him pull out his sawed-off shotgun. He grabbed my mother by her hair and marched her out the back door. He screamed for me and my brother to follow. He was cursing and calling her all sorts of nasty names, saying he was going to blow her head off and let it roll into the canal. He pushed my brother and me onto the ground. We were crying and pleading with him not to hurt her. He held the shotgun to her head as she lay on the ground, her head hanging off the edge, for what seemed like a long time. She pleaded for him to understand that we all needed to go back into the house. Suddenly he took her by the arm and yanked her from the ground. He yelled for all of us to get inside the house. The terror had stopped for that night.

The next day we spoke to our neighbor to let him know we were ready. He gave me the shotgun the following Friday, after our mother and stepfather left for the evening. When it was time for bed, I placed the shotgun under my bed where it wouldn't be visible if she came into the room.

We stayed awake that night for what seemed like forever and then we heard the car drive up. We knew what was about to happen next and what we planned to do. They came in as usual and went straight to their bedroom. We heard no talking, yelling, screaming, nothing. After about 10 minutes, we got up and tiptoed to their room door and put our ears to the door, still there was no sound. My brother and I looked at each other bewildered. We were too tired to talk about it and went back to bed.

The next day we were outside playing, when Mom, sounding angry, called for us to come inside. We followed her to my bedroom, where the shotgun had been placed on top of my bed. She screamed, "Why is this gun in my house?" I demand an explanation.

I explained, we were going to kill her husband for continually beating her. Her face grew sad as she looked at us. She said, "I'm sorry you thought to commit a murder because of my choices." She never bothered to have a conversation with us, as to why she allowed him to terrorize us and nearly kill her.

Throughout this turbulent time, we had a cousin who was close to my mother. She was the daughter of my mother's sister. She spent a lot of time with us until she went off to college and returned home married. When she learned of the abuse within our house, she was always feuding with my mother demanding to know, "Why? Why do you allow this to happen to you?" "Why do you stay in this marriage?"

On many occasions I would call her the day after the turbulent outbreaks, and she would rush over and rescue my brother and me. I remember her arguing with my mother again and then yelling for my brother and me to pack a bag, because we were leaving. In some way I felt protected by her when we left the area of rage. I felt relief from not having to witness another fight. But this relief was inconsistent, as our stepfather continued his reign of terror. A year later she divorced him.

The only positive thing I can say about my stepfather is that I learned how to cook and drive a car at the age of 12; but nothing else. I am also grateful that he never tried to molest me or touch me in any inappropriate way.

As I grew older, I concluded that my mother wanted to be and feel loved romantically, and her choices were men who were abusive physically. She remained single until we left home.

CHAPTER 3

Slackened to be Awakened

I graduated high school with a decent grade point average and decided to stay at home and attend the local junior college to pursue a nursing career. I found most of the basic college courses consistent with my high school courses easy, until I took anatomy and physiology. I had a tough time trying to read and memorize all of the bones in the body, all 206 of them. I began to feel overwhelmed and thought I would never pass that class.

The anxiety made me more overwhelmed. I thought, "I am not smart enough to pass this class." My understanding of anatomy and physiology was not there. I started to doubt my educational ability and started skipping class. At the end of the first semester, I had failed the course. I began to wonder if college was for me at all. Perhaps I should quit and get a job.

I continued to pretend I was going to college for the next semester, but I was hanging out with friends and seeking part time work. One day my mother approached me with a letter from the school. She was aware that I had dropped out. She expressed her disappointment and said I needed to find a job or move out of her home.

I went on the dating scene by hanging out with a few friends. I landed a job in a night club which gave me an opportunity to get out of my mom's house. The pay wasn't that great, but the tips were. By the time I was 16 years of age, I was five feet eight inches tall, with small perky breasts and I never wore a bra. My waistline was small, and I had large thighs and hips. While working in the club I met all types of men and the ones that hit on me the most, were affluent and educated. They were also married and that turned me on because there was no attachment.

I desired more money than what I was earning and most of the guys who showed interest were willing to give me money for sex. The other bar maids schooled me that being paid for sex was the quickest way to earn some extra money. But it wasn't long before I began to feel loneliness and despair. Most men stared at my body, especially my hips as though they were foreign to look at. The men only wanted to sleep with me as though I was a prostitute with big hips; that became obvious. But I was a lonely bar maid with no direction.

My first personal experience with domestic violence occurred when I hooked up with this guy I met right out of high school. He was tall, dark, and handsome - a lady's man. We met at a car tire shop, and we went on a few dates. I felt love toward him, and I thought he felt the same toward me.

The first incident was when he and I got into an in an argument about him seeing me with another guy. He accused me of hugging and kissing another person, which was a lie. He grabbed his TV from the dresser and threw it at me, while I was sitting on the bed.

I jumped up to dodge the TV and bent over to grab my clog shoe. I swung it and hit him in the mouth. The shoe split his bottom lip and blood flew everywhere, especially all over me. I ran out of the apartment and jumped into my car. I noticed I had no wounds. I felt fear, anger, betrayal, and rage as I thought, *A man can just attack for no reason.* I decided never to see him again.

Later on, I started dating an older married man I met at work. We were together for three years. I felt comfortable with his treatment of me, but still felt no fulfillment. He drove a nice car and showered me with gifts and money at times. One time he invited me to a six-week excursion to California. He had a part time summer job driving a tractor trailer. We left Florida in the truck and headed to California where he had to pick up a load of grapes. The trip seemed exhilarating, so I decided to journal the entire experience. I learned Texas was 1,000 miles across. No wonder it seemed like we were in Texas for a week.

I journaled the names of the different cities and the interesting sites I saw. At one point he wanted to teach me how to drive the truck, so I practiced in a large truck stop parking area. I'd learned to drive a standard shift car during my late teens, but it was no comparison to that big ten-wheeled machine. The enormity of it along with all of the gears was fascinating.

We continued on and when we reached Las Vegas, I was amazed by a 12-mile highway entirely lit up with varying colors. Some were still and others flashing. There were huge truck stops with small casinos in them. I had no gambling experience, but it was fun to observe the excitement of others.

Being with him for this duration allowed me to ask questions about his private life. I asked about his wife and child. He was reluctant at first, but soon opened up. He had been married for 15 years, had an older daughter from his first marriage and an eight-year-old from his second marriage. This trip was magical, beautiful and something I'd not experienced with any man. I thought I deserved more from a romantic relationship and let him know my feelings. I had developed feelings while dating him, that made me feel vulnerable and lonely when we were not together.

He said he understood, and thought he could make our relationship work, giving me most of his spare time. It was not the kind of loving relationship I wanted.

We never spoke about it again until the day he dropped me at the airport in New York. I was going home, and he would continue his run for six more weeks. He admitted he had no intentions of leaving his wife and that he thought I was okay with him being married. The relationship was over.

I worked two jobs and was a party girl with no children, no money, and no purpose. I was wild and troubled. I was an alcoholic and partied all over town. There were many instances that I would be out partying on a night I was scheduled to work and would call in sick to keep partying. I felt since I had no one close to me, children nor spouse that the people I knew in the street were better to hang out with than being at home alone. I had a lot of friends in a lot of places that were no good for me. They either wanted to use me or have sex with me.

I continued this shaky path but was able to save enough money to buy the car of my dreams. A prized 1978 Pontiac Trans AM. It was brand new and black with black leather interior. It had the big golden eagle on the hood with the exhaust sticking out of the middle. It also had large wheels shaped like honeycombs and Tee tops.

I washed it every week and was in love with it. I drove it with pride and wouldn't let anyone ride in it. It was mine. It made me feel superior to those who marveled at it. That car made me feel like I was somebody. As unstable as my life was, so was my finances. I was often late with mortgage payments and had been served eviction notices. I managed to play catch up every few months. This staved off final foreclosure. I was also three months behind on the car note, which occurred often. One morning I awakened to find it had been re-possessed.

Soon after, I found myself on the verge of being fired. I worked at an insurance agency as a clerk during the day and a bar maid at night. While I continued to abuse alcohol and drugs, I became even more depressed. I called in sick more often which, I knew could lead to job termination

I once allowed a couple of friends to rent a room in my townhome in an effort to make more money. They never paid; they just ripped me off. They made many excuses month after month about why they could not pay the rent. I saw how gullible and lonely I was. Finally, I had them escorted out of my home.

I became sick and tired of the way I was living. My depression, worsened, and I had thoughts of suicide often and tried to end my life. I took a bottle of pills one night when I was home alone feeling as though I had no one and nothing to live for. A friend, who had a key, stopped by to hang out and found me unresponsive.

A trip to the emergency department and a pumped stomach made me feel no better about myself.

Left without a vehicle to get to work, I felt I had run out of options. I had become a bus rider, which made me wonder if my mom would help me out.

Even though our relationship became estranged after quitting college, I knew she thought the world of me and would often remark that she thought I could be a good nurse. She only wanted what was best for me, but I could not see that. I randomly mentioned one day that I was looking for employment and inquired about opportunities where she worked. My mother was a supervisor at a large mental health facility, and she agreed to walk me through the employment process. A few weeks later I was hired for the evening shift.

CHAPTER 4

New Awakenings

While working the 3:00pm to 11:00 pm shift, I was introduced to my supervisor. The staff called him JC There were times I would notice him staring at me. It felt different than the way other men looked at me.

At first, I didn't find him attractive, but I realized the encounters with him made me feel different about myself. I felt pretty, uplifted and interesting. He continued his flirting but not in an unethical manner. I thought, wow he is digging me. This type of optimistic forward movement had never happened before. My past relationship left me feeling that a man simply wanted me for sex, eventually. Most would not be open about how they felt about me. I remembered those men coming on to me loaded with their negative comments such as, "Wow your ass is big" or "How about you break me off a piece of that."

The encounters with JC were different. He spoke to me in such an uplifting manner. It was as if he was seducing me in a respectable way. He demonstrated attraction to me that I had never felt before. The feeling gave me hope to fix my life by getting into a relationship I desired.

I began coming to work on time each day primarily to see him. I went out and bought a new wardrobe with clothes that were professional but also seductive to my body shape. I began hanging around him during break time and loving the attention I was receiving. He continued to comment on my work performance and tell me how smart I was.

The comments made me feel special. Someone was finally paying me attention. His attention and the emotions it stirred definitely lifted some of my depression. I was less lonely and began gaining the confidence to live better.

One night, the entire night shift (three people) called in sick. JC asked me to work overtime with him to cover the shift. Of course, I agreed, I was delighted. Eight more hours with him would give me an opportunity to learn about him. Who is he? Where is he from? What was his relationship life like, family, etc.,

After we did the rounds and filled out the required paperwork, we relaxed in the nursing station. This allowed us time to get to know each other a little more. Although I had been working with him on the prior shift, I did not have the opportunity to look at him and really observe him physically. He had brown eyes and a receding hairline. His teeth were pearly white and looked as though he had once worn braces. His body was slender and fit, but his charisma knocked me out within. He spoke soft and deep and began asking questions about my past. He asked why I had no children. I told him I was too young and not ready for children, nor could I afford to be a single parent.

Silently, I remembered a situation with my own upbringing. When I started to menstruate around the age of 13, my mother sat me down and said these words. "Now that you are of age to have a period, you must be extra careful, never to let a boy touch you in any way sexual. If he penetrates your vagina with his penis, you might very well get pregnant. I'm a single mother to you and your brother and I would not be able to support another child. You and your child would not be able to stay here. I remained a virgin until I was 17 years of age.

During sex health classes at school, I was made aware of a pregnancy prevention clinic in the community. I visited the clinic and while filling out the papers, one line stated, sign here if you agree that you are at high risk for getting pregnant. I signed there because by then I was curious and wanted to have sex. Next there was a physical and vaginal exam and birth control pills were prescribed.

I remembered another lecture my mother gave me when I was 10. It was about being aware of child molesters. The conversation came up because she was escorting my brother and me to a coming home party for my uncle, my father's brother. Though they were divorced, Mom brought us to the party so we could spend some time with our father.

She said the following words with a fierce sounding voice and an ugly look on her face. "You see your uncle over there? His brother, your father and stepmother are throwing him a coming home party. He was away in prison, for molesting his twin daughters, how absurd. If any man ever approaches you and touches you in an inappropriate way, you are to run away from them and tell an adult what happened in case you can't reach me first. Do you understand?"

I've carried those words in my heart and mind my whole life. The way she sounded gave me chills. Those memories filled my mind. I responded, "I don't think I want any children."

Later as JC and I continued to talk about our lives, He told me that he was in a relationship but was not married. He had a two-year-old son from the relationship he was involved with at the time, and he was quite happy with his son. He said he had been married once before for five years but was divorced, which produced his first son.

He went on to say "The relationship is bad. She is unwilling to work. She has no diploma and won't go back to school." He continued holding me and said, "I seem to have a habit of picking up women who don't want anything out of life." He went on to say his marriage with his first wife ended because she also was uneducated, had a few children from a couple of different men. He left that relationship and went on to the same type of relationship as the first one. He then smiled, looking at me lovingly and said, jokingly "That was not really me, but obviously one of my personalities."

While working another night shift with JC, he began telling me about his upbringing. He grew up in Tampa, Florida, a city near central Florida, and was raised in the Seventh Day Adventist religion. He had gone to junior college and graduated in a year with his associate degree. He went to school later on to get his bachelor's degree but dropped out when he got married to his first wife. He said he had dreamed of getting a doctorate degree at some point in his life.

I made myself stay awake that night to listen intently to this guy who seemed to have his priorities in place and that pleased me even more. I was a little wary of getting into a relationship with him, because of the woman he was living with and the fact that he had a 2-year-old son. I decided our relationship would be casual only.

Even though I had dated married men before, this un-married man touched my heart strings. In a lot of ways, he was like a father figure who was proud of his daughter. He often took a moment while working to comment on my beauty, saying "You are beautiful. Do you know that?" or "That lipstick you are wearing today looks beautiful with your skin color." These types of comments I had never heard. It was all so arousing, it made me feel tingly inside and I could only think about him. Considering what a great guy he was, our causal relationship did not last long. I was falling in love and as my co-workers would say, it was obvious to everyone at work.

One night I gave him a ride home and when we arrived, he reached over and gave me a kiss. Wow the stars burst inside of me. It felt like butterflies were all around as well as the stars. I could not contain myself. I think we both knew there was something brewing between us, but that kiss was as powerful as a nuclear bomb.

The next day I was so anxious to get to work, I went in early, even though he was not there yet, to look at him. My longing to see him was overwhelming. When he arrived, he smiled that beautiful smile and acted professionally to carry on his duties. We caught each other looking at one another many times that evening. Later he asked if he could speak with me in private on our dinner break and I lovingly said yes.

During dinner he announced he was breaking off his relationship with his girlfriend, because all she wanted was to be financially cared for by someone and have babies. He told me his girlfriend announced that she was pregnant shortly before he left for work that day.

He said he told his parents just before arriving to work and lamented on how he could not trust her. They both had agreed that they would get back in school, and she would take the birth control pills they had gotten from Planned Parenthood.

He said he told them that as soon as the baby was born, he would take her and the two children to her mother's home in another part of the state. He said he had shared this information with the girlfriend's mother, and she agreed to let her live back at home. I thought this guy is serious about his future and seemed quite responsible for the children he has now and was making provisions to financially care for the new baby as well.

The day came when the child with his ex-girlfriend was born. By that time, JC and I were a couple. The baby boy was only two weeks old when, as he said he would, he drove his ex-girlfriend and their two children back home to be with her mother.

I believed the respect and love I had for JC was real. I had no memory of the men I'd dated before exhibiting these behaviors. This sensation for JC was full of energy and I desired more.

When he arrived back in town, I was glad he made the trip safely. He came directly to my home, and we made passionate love in a warm and quiet environment. We were both off from work that day and we lay around exploring each other in intimate ways. We stared into each other's eyes and said nothing. He held me so close I could feel his heartbeat as one with mine. My eros love was on fire.

In a disappointing turn of events, my townhouse was lost in foreclosure. JC assisted me in a search for a new place, which presented an opportunity for us to move in together and which we did.

He quickly established the monthly support payments to the mother of his two estranged children. As he set this practice in motion, I had an Aha moment. Here I am in love with a man who seems to care more about his kids than my own father cared for my brother and me. At least even if JC did not have constant contact with his children, their mother would have his financial support to see her through.

I remember asking my mother at some point in my life if our father ever gave her child support? She replied, "Not one red cent." She added, "I did not even bother to go to the courts to get child support, because I knew he would never pay it." I didn't see this behavior in JC, I thought of him as a real father, because he chose first to pay the mother of his children for their care.

Our relationship was pure bliss. We were so in love. We took our days off to take walks in the rain, go to the beach often, especially at night. There were very few people on the beach at night. We were free to lie down and be with each other.

We made love in the car, which I'd never done before, and the experience elevated me to a level of satisfaction with myself and the choices I was making about my dating life. We always talked and he would allow me to express any and everything. He listened intently as always to my life problems. He was a shoulder to cry on as he sometimes gave me simple advice. He never judged me in any of my many faults.

I didn't have friends that I felt comfortable with talking about my personal life. They were just the party type of friend, as was I. My mother and I had an estranged relationship, because she always accused me of dropping out of nursing school and I was sick of hearing it. She knew I abused drugs and alcohol, and she was not happy with my lifestyle. It never sat right with her.

I never told anyone about this new relationship and only our co-workers knew we had become inseparable. One night while at work on our late break, he talked me into climbing the fire escape to the roof. He brought up a couple of towels for us to sit on. Soon he was touching my breast as I made my way out of my pants. We made love under clear skies, full of stars on that roof. I felt genuinely loved.

He felt like a father figure as he strategically encouraged me to start saving money. He asked me to take a look at my own income. He taught me how to make a budget. This would help us work with our finances together as a couple. I began to realize that I've never experienced even a father that taught me any of these things. JC remained loving and encouraging in every aspect of my life.

He was interested in dialogue on how I may have mismanaged my finances. He would speak gently when asking me about how I felt about my life. I replied, "I have hope for a better future."

He remarked "Jenny you are smarter than you know. Your innate abilities are within and soon you will begin to see your potential." I recognized that JC was smart and willing to be with me.

We were speaking one day about his three sons, and how he needed to go to the Department of Children and Families in Florida to set up a payment plan for the last two children. He said he was beginning to miss them and wanted to do the right thing regarding their support.

The oldest son was in the shared custody of his first wife and child support was set up at the time of their divorce. All of his payments had been on time, and he cared for this this son during the summer. He was sorting out his new life with me, which made me love him more. He was methodical and detailed at orchestrating it all.

We would occasionally take time to drive to Tampa so he could spend time with his mother and stepfarther. I was given many opportunities to get to know them. They were in their late 70s and had been married for 20 years. This was the 2nd marriage for both of them. His mother was a small woman in stature with leathery black skin. She moved around slowly, semi hunched over. On the other hand, his stepfather was tall, brown skinned and always smiling, He seemed quiet but inquisitive. His mother was the talkative one. On one occasion she asked if I loved her son, and I replied yes. She said she could tell so by our interactions. She was pleased that he seemed happier.

CHAPTER 5

Leaving Home

After a year of living together, he asked me to move to Tampa with him so he could be near his mother and stepfather. His mother was suffering from a heart condition, and he wanted to spend more time with her. I was unsure about the move. I had been in Miami my whole life. I had visited other places, but I never thought of moving away.

I visited my mother to tell her about our plans. I told her how much I had fallen in love and wanted to spend every waking moment with JC. The thought of not being with him was saddening. I told her I was anxious about moving to a different environment, but I wanted to try it out. She gave me her blessing and said, "I'm just a phone call away."

We packed up our wares and quit our jobs on the same day. We had a little money, but I was still afraid and unsure of this change. Yet, as the time grew closer for the move, I discovered how I began to feel safe, empowered and connected to JC. I couldn't consider living without him.

We found a small two-bedroom, one bathroom house nestled under a huge oak tree with an open carport in the local newspaper. It felt like a small country home. We fixed it up with new window curtains, new bathroom fixtures, outside lighting and our furniture we hauled from home. We were happy.

After we moved to Tampa, JC opened up to me about his mental health challenges, his history with incarceration, his first marriage, his first son, the breakup of his marriage, and his move back home. He struggled with attention deficit disorder for many years when he was young. He remembers his childhood was filled with going to see many psychiatrists, because he was always moving and running around. He had been given strong medication with the hope of changing his behavior. He spoke of nights that he was unable to sleep and thought of suicide. There were so many thoughts racing and raging in his mind, he could not control his impulses. It seemed no one knew how to treat a young person with this disorder in his younger years. He had also been diagnosed schizophrenic.

The worst of the malady came with an angry outburst toward his mother. He was always getting into trouble at school for not following the rules. A teacher once said to him, "Oh what a tangle web we weave when first we practice to deceive."

The paranoia of others talking or plotting to harm him scared me. I wondered how such a beautiful person could function in today's society with this type of illness. I kept quiet about those thoughts, so as not to make things worse. Once I witnessed his insomnia when he stayed awake for a full 24 hours. I suffer from chronic insomnia, in which I could easily fall asleep, but any noise or movement of others would awaken me. This particular night he was in and out of bed or watching TV. Throughout the night. I managed to go back to sleep each time.

When I finally awakened that morning, he was sitting up in bed observing me. I asked, "Did you get any sleep?" His response was a sad no. I highlighted that he had been awake for 27 hours. He then explained that he never gets enough sleep because of the constant voices in his head. He can control it only a fraction of the time. At this point I had a moment of serious consideration about who I had fallen in love with.

CHAPTER 6

Transitioning

During breakfast he shared more about his past. He mentioned that just before his high school graduation, the boys he had been in a gang with, robbed and killed a man. He was later charged as an accessory to that crime because the prosecutor said he knew about the robbery and did not tell the authorities. He denied he knew anything. With remorse in his voice, he shared, "I didn't know this gang of boys would ever stoop to robbery and murder, which haunts me to this day." He was held in the county jail for a year due to his age and later sent to a penitentiary.

He graduated high school while incarcerated with a GED. He was asked by the staff to teach the other inmates how to study for the test. It was then that he met a guy (also from Florida), whose name was WB. They began talking about their shared interests and how they grew up. One day WB received a letter from his mother. When WB was attempting to read the letter, JC noticed he was stumbling through simple words and had difficulty putting the sentences together. He asked WB if he could read the letter to him? WB admitted, "I never learned to read. I dropped out of school while in the 7th grade."

JC read the letter to him. Later on, he found out that WB dropped out of school to sell drugs. They became close as JC began tutoring his new friend daily. After two years of time served, they were allowed to go to a minimum-security prison if they promised to be supervised and attend the local junior college. By this time, WB was reading college level books thanks to JC's help. They were both happy to get out of the penitentiary.

Needless to say, they both had to adhere to the rules. They were bused to the local junior college daily and allowed library time after classes and on Saturdays. They managed to graduate with a two-year degree in one year. They then both entered Florida Memorial College to work on a bachelor's degree in criminology.

During his time at Florida Memorial College, JC met his first wife. He said she was an older woman with a lot of wisdom, He noted that he had been incarcerated since the age of 16 and never been in a relationship. He recalled the relationship was beautiful but different because he saw her as a mother figure. He spent a lot of time with her and her family on the weekends. He also met and connected several times with WB's family who adopted him as one of their own. His relationship with his girlfriend moved fast. She wanted him out of the minimum-security prison and thought they should marry. Because JC and WB had done so well in the minimum-security prison, they were placed on probation and allowed to leave the facility.

His girlfriend asked him to move into her home, with her and her three boys. He had met the boys on a few occasions when he was allowed out of the facility. He also met his girlfriends' mother and her sisters. Because of the incarceration he had nowhere else to go. He continued his studies at Florida Memorial College, until his girlfriend propositioned him to move to Atlanta Georgia. She said she had more relatives there, and they were living better lives. She told him there would be a place for them to stay, the home of one of her uncles. She also told him that he would also be able to work for the largest Ford manufacturing plant, which paid good money. He pondered her offer, but wondered about school, he had a desire for a degree. He later relented and off to Georgia they went.

Just as she promised, they settled into her uncle's home and the uncle got him a position with Ford Motor Corporation where he was earning more money than he ever had. He had been incarcerated since the age of 16 and had never worked. Soon they were married and later that year his first child - a son - was born and named after him.

During their late-night conversation, JC and his then wife shared more of their history. JC let her know his birth certificate said he was born in Georgia, but his memories are only of living in Tampa Florida. Being in Atlanta made him feel as though he may have been adopted and born somewhere in Georgia. They spoke of this sounding odd but had no proof of their conspiracy theories. He noted that his aunt, his mother's sister, and his mother both had adopted children. In fact, they adopted two babies at the same time.

His wife assured him that she would look through county records to see what she could find. She uncovered that his place of birth was in Duluth Georgia. They were eager to travel to Duluth to see it and possibly look at some of the county records. Soon they had a weekend trip to the Southern city where they uncovered the name of one person who possibly knew JC's mother's family, based on her maiden name. They came to a local restaurant and went in to have lunch. They asked the owners if they had heard of a family with her last name. They were told there were a couple of families living nearby with that last name and told them where they could find them.

The man was instrumental in giving them the name of a particular family that lived nearby. They visited with this family, but did not find any new information, however JC started to notice during their travel to this town that there were some people that resembled him. They decided not to push the matter and returned home. He was so proud to be a father. Married life gave him stability as did becoming a parent. Unfortunately, the marriage ended after two years. He felt lost and abandoned in Atlanta and moved back to Florida to his parents' home. He spoke of his journey back home. He settled in with his mother and stepfather. They had agreed to take him back home again. They were glad he was no longer incarcerated. He re-connected with his cousins, Gail, and Robert. He recalls the three of them were close as teenagers.

He started to look for work and found a mental health technician position in neighboring Saint Petersburg. It was a live-in position for low functioning male teenagers. He told me how he felt exhilarated on the other side of incarceration, after seeing how those boys had to live. He started exploring the community and found the beaches beautiful. He would go swimming on his off days. It was there that he met his two boys' mother. He said, "she was dark, beautiful and radiant, like a Nubian Queen."

He fell in love at first sight. He spoke of their migration to Miami, because he found a better position and had a desire to finish his bachelor's degree at Florida Memorial College.

CHAPTER 7

Our New Beginning

One year after moving to Tampa, we were married in the open carport of our home, under our big oak tree. We were poor; my dress was bought from a consignment shop for $20.00 and JC rented a tuxedo with those ugly plastic leather looking shoes. We laughed until we cried at the thought of pulling off this "poor man's wedding," as he referred to it as. My mom bought the wedding rings and flew from Miami to Tampa for the wedding. My cousin who had rescued us from mayhem as children, came with her husband and their daughter. My brother and sister-in-law came with their first child.

JC's cousins and neighbors were excited for us. They volunteered a pastor to officiate the service and brought in other family members to set up and decorate the carport. One of our neighbors catered and set up light refreshments. The collaboration of people known, and unknown was magical. I felt like Cinderella. While JC and I were in the bedroom, we were hugging and kissing while getting dressed. I giggly spoke about my nervousness and my thoughts of making a mistake in marrying him. I fell into his arms crying and told him how his presence in my life meant the world to me. I was a changed woman and ready to take a leap.

I yelled "Let's do this."

He said, "Hell yea! I love you and want you in my life forever."

I knew JC needed some time away to think through his decision to marry me. He had been out until after midnight, the night before. I asked him where he went the night before. He said he had taken time to visit with the mother of his two boys and give her the news. He thought it was the right thing to do. She became angry and yelled as he tried to hug her.

She hit him on his back repeatedly, asking, "Why, why are you marrying her?"

She then vowed that he would never see his boys again. He said he told her that he was certain he was making the right decision for his life. He told her he would always be there for her and the boys, no matter what. I was thankful that he shared this information with me, his soon to be wife.

The time came to do the ceremony. His cousins served as his best man and my maid of honor. JC walked out after them and waited near the best man. I soon came out with my rose bouquet smiling as I approached him. The pastor did his routine service speech and soon we were exchanging vows and rings. That queasy, butterfly sensation I felt when he first kissed me was back. I wanted to melt.

Finally, the pastor said, "You may kiss the bride." And we kissed for what seemed like eternity, as the crowd stood and clapped.

Other attendees started to serve food that had also been set up on the porch. Everyone seemed happy and gleeful to attend our nuptials. The photographer asked us to go under the oak tree to take some photos. Afterwards we mingled with family and friends. There was no honeymoon, so my cousins took us all out for dinner. JC got an extended opportunity to bond with my immediate family. That made me happy that he would be a part of my small family.

Two days later, JC got down to business. He awakened me with the smell of bacon. As I entered the kitchen, he was smiling and said, "Let's eat. We have to get to the local college and get you enrolled for classes, so you can finish your nursing degree." I thought *OMG what is going on here? I've not set foot in a school in years,* surely, I could not fathom what to expect.

I began to see how efficiently he operated. He was always in contact with the mother of his eldest son. The conversation included the fact that he was now remarried. I overheard a conversation he was having with the mother of the girlfriend with two children. He let her know he had gotten married and visited with her daughter and the boys, the night before the wedding. He assured her that he would send funds monthly to support the children. He said he would contact her monthly, if possible. He let her know that her daughter threatened to never allow him to see the children.

He stated, "Maybe she will find a way to forgive me."

I was now enrolled in college full time, taking the basic courses needed for a degree. My husband was scouting for a position as an insurance agent. He sat for the Florida State board Life-Health insurance exam. He passed without even reading the manuals. Soon he took a position as a life insurance agent with Atlanta Life Insurance.

Married life grew different quickly. I began to notice that my husband had become possessive. He even started telling me what to wear. One time we were invited to a friend's house for dinner. This guy was someone he had gone to school with but had not been in contact with for a while.

I put on a nice pants set I'd worn before, but he sternly commented as he pointed to a dress in the closet, "That dress would be more appropriate for this outing, not the pantsuit."

I'd never seen that behavior before. I remained quiet to keep down any friction. This was tough for me. I had been single and on my own for quite some time. I was not used to being treated that way by any man. I tried to blend in with his interpretation of a good marriage. We spent most of our free time together. We went to the beach in Saint Petersburg most Saturdays. He loved to swim while I walked along the shallow part. He would tell me stories about his short time living here. We would finish with big cheeseburgers from his favorite beach side restaurants.

His parents would visit almost every Sunday and bring dinner. One Sunday, I encouraged him, to confront his mother, about him being possibly adopted and he agreed. We all gathered around the dinner table, to hold hands in prayer. We sat down and began to eat. I was a little nervous as to the timing he would confront his mother. We finished dinner and I went to the kitchen to begin cleaning up. They settled in the living room. I soon joined them.

He said, "Mother, I want to ask you a question." She acknowledged his statement. He asked, "Was I adopted?"

She looked shocked by the question. She bowed her head, folded her hands, and became still and speechless. An answer later emerged from her in a soft monotone manner. She answered, "You are my child and I've had you since you were six weeks old, and I have loved and cared for you, your whole life."

She became quiet again and offered no other information. By this time JC was bent forward in tears. I could do no more than try to console him.

His stepfather soon asked, "Lizzie, JC was adopted? You never told me." His mother and stepfather soon left in a hurry.

One weekend we went out for lobster dinner and upon arrival we noticed the restaurant was filled with Caucasians and no Black people. I could feel my husband's emotions rising and see it in the look on his face. He had once remarked that Tampa was still a racist city, and that he did not like White people. It was becoming clear that we were going to have a problem.

We were greeted by the host and taken to our seats. I soon began to hear voices from the table next to us. A group of White men talking negatively about Black people coming to the restaurant. I asked my husband to please ignore the rhetoric and let's enjoy some lobster. Soon I noticed he was easing his feet out of his shoes. I grabbed his hand and asked what he was about to do.

He said loudly, "I'm going kick their asses!"

Immediately I stood up and yelled "MANAGER," and thankfully he came running quickly. I let him know of the racial slurs coming from the table next to us. He went over and without apology asked them all to leave his restaurant. I was relieved. He returned to apologize to us, but my husband was already greatly upset.

He said, "We will not be eating in here."

We left and I asked where we would eat now.

He said, "We are going home."

I insisted we find another restaurant because I was hungry. A 30-minute argument ensued. He yelled that I should stay in my place, and I should have not yelled for the manager, he wanted to "kill those crackers" because he saw how they flexed at me when we passed by them. He yelled that I had better stay out of his business. I had never seen that behavior of him before.

I was being dominated and controlled. I was witnessing frightening anger and rage I had not seen in him before either. His unpredictable behaviors emerged. One day we were arguing about something, I don't remember what it was, while he was ironing clothes. Suddenly he slammed the iron on the ironing board repeatedly as he was yelling. He slammed it so hard; the iron broke into pieces and the ironing board crashed to the floor. I was frightened out of my wits, and I became afraid of him. In the two years we had dated and lived together, sure we had some arguments, but I had never seen that sort of explosive behavior before.

We had gone out for drinks on another occasion and when we got home an argument ensued. He became enraged and I ran into the bathroom. He kicked in the door opened, grabbed me by the spaghetti strap dress and yanked me toward him. The yanking of the dress left cuts on my shoulders. Those cuts went down into the white meat of my skin. I was terrified. There would be many arguments about money, bills, and spending (I was never good at either). This really aggravated the relationship. Domestic violence was off to a raging start as a new partner in our marriage. I felt trapped. By the end of our first anniversary, I no longer wanted to be married.

My mother called to wish me a happy anniversary. I stated, "It's not happy at all." I confided in her that I made a mistake and never should have married him. She asked me what was going on and I started to cry then sob uncontrollably. She held the phone in silence, allowing me time to gather myself.

I shared the violent verbal and physical abuse as well as the unwarranted outbursts. I felt lonely away from home and was afraid to have any conversations with him. When he became angry about anything, I would not say a word, for fear of his rage. I felt silenced and couldn't see myself staying in the marriage any longer.

CHAPTER 8

Unfulfillment

I stayed for 20 years. I told myself, at least I had a husband that brought a stable environment as far as our infrastructure. I thought for sure, if I just follow his rules, dummy down myself from the vocal and in control person I used to be, everything would be okay. I was afraid to go back to my familiar home. I still had not yet finished college and that had been a dream from the age of nine. I stayed because I did not want to be alone. Loneliness brought me anguish, despair, depression, and the feeling that no one wanted me. At least I was married.

I believed in us – somehow. I accepted his anger, rage, and domestic violence because that is what I witnessed from my stepfather. I was in deep fear. This is what happens to women. I began to lean on my mother for support and advice. We spoke weekly.

She asked me what was my decision to stay, not the reason. I shared that I decided to stay in my marriage to keep some sort of stability for myself. She advised it was not her place to tell me what to do. Even though there was domestic violence involved, she would not tell me what I should do with my marriage. She said, "I would be out of line."

She began telling me about her life with our father, which I had never heard her talk about in any detail. She remarked that many years ago he had us in the car as little children and was arrested for driving down the grassy divider in the highway. She mentioned another incident where she came home from work and found him passed out behind the wheel of the car. She stated he was abusive to her on many occasions and during one of his outbursts, threw my brother, aged 15 months, across the room where he hit the wall and fell to the floor screaming. She remarked she had no choice but to have him admitted to a hospital for severe alcoholism. He stayed a few days and was released with a prescription called Disulfiram which was used to treat the disease. He took it for a few weeks, but then relapsed and started drinking heavily again. It was at this time she had no choice but to leave him.

Much later, after my brother and me had finished high school and moved on, Mom remarried a third time. I was still living in Tampa and saw her on occasion. I met her new husband once. He seemed like a good man for her. He worked for the airline, and they enjoyed going on cruises and traveling. After about two years into my marriage, there was a family reunion on my maternal side in Tallahassee, and my husband and I agreed to attend. At this point, I had not seen my mother in about a year. As we were checking into the hotel, I caught a glimpse of her getting out of her car. She was traveling alone. As we moved closer to one another, I noticed she had a black eye. I immediately asked what had happened.

She said, "I can't talk about it." I asked for her room number and if I could escort her there. She agreed.

After getting her settled and unpacked, I asked again about her injury. She commented that she could not talk about it. I looked her in the eye and asked, "You have come to this family reunion that you helped to fund with a black eye, and you refuse to speak about it? What will the family say when they observe this?"

She began crying and I hugged her. As she began to feel less tense in my arms, she said, "if I tell anyone about my injury, he will kill your brother."

I quickly stepped back and asked, "What on Earth are you saying?"

She explained, "My husband and I were embroiled in an argument, and he hit me several times leaving me with this black eye." She told me as she was preparing to come to the reunion, he commented in a threatening manner that she better not tell my brother, (whom at the time worked as a federal officer), or he would kill him. We hugged and sobbed, and I promised not to tell her secret. I could feel she believed him, and I wanted her to feel my love.

Entering the next year of our marriage JC tried to be civil with the mother of his two younger sons, but she was resistant. We would send toys and clothing by mail for Christmas, birthdays, and Easter, which would come back marked "Return to sender". This hurt him in a profound way. He had sadness written all over him, and he looked defeated with no way out. I felt concerned for his emotional health and wondered if his violence toward me would pick up. He continued to have verbal outburst, but the fighting died down. After 3 years of marriage, he asked if I would see a fertility doctor to see if there was any chance that I could conceive a child.

CHAPTER 9

Moving On

At the age of 20, three years before meeting my husband, I had surgery to remove dermoid cysts from my ovaries. These cysts were not cancerous but had the propensity to get large. The one I had was the size of a grapefruit. I was told it might be difficult to conceive children because the cysts were so big. The ovary and fallopian tube on the left side were removed and only a portion of the ovary and fallopian tube were spared on the right side

I carried this information into my marriage but thought my husband would not want any more children, since he had three. I agreed to see a fertility specialist in September of 1985. The doctor performed a series of tests and requested I undergo a scope test under anesthesia to reveal the ovaries.

On the subsequent visit he revealed I had a small quantity of cysts on the ovary on the right and virtually none on the left side. He agreed to take me on as a new patient after the Christmas holidays and see if I could be a candidate for invitro fertilization.

We traveled to Miami to spend Christmas with my mother and to spend time with old friends. By Christmas day, I began to feel listless and weak. I had no appetite and standing made me feel even worse. It was quick, random, and weird as though I had come down with the flu or perhaps mononucleosis. As a nurses aide I recognized some of the symptoms I'd witnessed while working in the hospital. My breasts hurt like never before. My husband decided we go to see the fertility doctor as soon as we got back home.

We were able to get an appointment just before the new year and were eager to see what the doctor would say. After the doctor examined me, he asked for a urine sample. I thought, *"Why would he want a urine sample?"* I was curious about the need for a urine test, but I obliged. He re-emerged approximately 10 minutes later smiling; and announced that I was pregnant. All of this news three years into marriage.

Quickly a wave of happy and sad tears erupted.

The doctor asked, "Why the tears?"

I replied, "I was told I may never have children and that is what I prepared my life to be- childless!"

My husband was ecstatic, jumping up and down, exclaiming "I remember the day I made this baby." I looked at him in disdain.

We received this information on December 30th, so our New Year's Eve was unlike any other. No smoking, drinking, or partying. We threw out cigarettes, wine, beer, and liquor. We watched the New Year's Eve festivities on TV without our usual fanfare. The Super Bowl festivities were equally weird, no smoking, drinking, or partying. The best thing was the domestic violence stopped.

Once I started going to the OBGYN monthly, my husband accompanied me. He was worried about the pregnancy, because it had been next to impossible for me to conceive in the first place. He would sit with me in the exam room until the test to detect the babies' heart rate was successful, and then he would leave the room. This continued for 7 months.

The pregnancy was tough. I was always nauseous and had little to no appetite for food or water. I knew the baby and I needed nutrients, so I would attempt to eat breakfast and drink milk, which came back up every time. The smell of fried food, cigarette smoke and money made me vomit. My lower back ached so bad I would sit on a pillow wherever I went.

It was exhilarating knowing I was pregnant. But I questioned how it happened. I had no knowledge of these feelings. It was interesting to watch my belly grow with a line coming from my breast downward. To feel this entity inside of me was uplifting. I began to talk to the baby, especially when it began to move, early in the mornings.

I would say "Good morning. I wonder what you look like?" I loved classical music and played it often. I would read aloud hoping he baby would hear the words. These things brought me peace.

We chose not to know the sex of our baby. We prayed for a healthy baby and considering the circumstances, which was good enough. I visited the doctor during my sixth month and found out I was not gaining enough weight. I had complained to this doctor on numerous occasions, how sick I felt all of the time.

He stated, "There were no medicines to make me feel better, because they could harm the baby." At the time of delivery, I had only gained 8 pounds.

On July 31st we went to buy a bassinet and other items the baby would need. I was nine months and smothering in the heat of July. I asked my husband jokingly, how we could make this baby come on out!

As we got our items and approached the car, warm clear liquid ran down my legs through my panties and into my shoes. I stood still and yelled, "Oh my God, my water just broke."

He ran to the car's trunk looking for a towel for me to sit on. We rushed home so I could change clothes and pack a bag. There was a sense of elation for both of us. We were preparing for the arrival of our baby, and it was time! He called the doctor's office, and we were instructed to go to the hospital.

When we arrived home, I quickly changed clothes and went into the bathroom to fix my hair. I had a beautiful Jeri curl at the time. I stood in the mirror and said to myself, "Okay, you must look your best before you go to the hospital." I sprayed the hair lotion and spritzer on my hair and arranged it in a presentable style. I then began to apply makeup.

My husband stormed into the bathroom and asked, "What are you doing?" I had a moment of fear, remembering when he had kicked in this same bathroom door a couple of years prior, to attack me while we were embroiled in an argument.

"I'm fixing up myself," I replied.

He said, "Are you crazy? Your water has broken, and we need to get to the hospital NOW!"

I thought, *what if something happened to me, I could possibly die and no matter what, I would like to look my best.* I remarked, "Please give me a few minutes to look presentable. It's important to me."

I could see the anxiety in him. Surely, he was concerned about the baby. He left me alone and calmed down. As he exited, I assured him that we would get to the hospital soon.

Once we arrived at the hospital I was in no pain, but eager to deliver this baby. We had requested a private room in advance of the delivery. I was pushed in a wheelchair as my husband tagged along, with all of my belongings in his arms.

I was placed in a hospital bed in a beautiful room, dolled up to look like a bedroom. As I perused the room, there was a baby warming bassinet behind a curtain near the window. There was another area in a corner with a curtain draped to look like a window, but there was other medical equipment behind it. I thought, *okay at least it looks quiet and serene for childbirth*. I was examined and hooked up to all sorts of electronic equipment. The nurse started an intravenous infusion of saline. The most important piece of equipment was the internal fetal heart monitor, a portion of which would be placed into the baby's scalp.

The doctor finally arrived, looked at the reports and advised I had dilated only two centimeters and 10 was the number needed for a successful vaginal birth. I felt disappointed because with the water break, I thought things would soon speed up. The nurse asked me to try and relax and assured me she would check on me often.

Over the next four hours, I was checked and found to only have dilated one more centimeter. I was disappointed and saw the anguish on my husband's face. Dilating from 3 to 10 seemed like it would take an eternity. Since it was my pregnancy, I did not know what to expect. The nurse said she would notify the doctor. She came back and reported the doctor ordered an IV infusion called Pitocin. This drug helps to speed up dilation of the cervix for childbirth. My husband and I agreed to allow the infusion.

After 20 minutes of this drug, I began to experience violent vaginal and deep back pain. I was starting to have contractions. I thought the process would continue to advance in an easy manner. But the contraction was coming every 3-5 minutes. Thirty minutes of this sent me into sheer terror. The pain was so intense, it felt like lightning bolts were hitting my womb and I could do nothing to control or slow it down. After 1 hour I begged my husband to get the nurse. I became angry and wanted the pain to STOP.

In the third trimester, we had taken birthing classes for two weeks. The instructor never spoke about Pitocin and the violent contractions this medicine could produce. I felt blindsided, dismayed, and ran amuck. I thought I would be able to sue the hospital.

When the nurse came in to check, I had dilated eight centimeters. I felt like the progression was too fast. I asked for pain medicine but was denied because it was not good for the baby. I cried out, "What about me?"

The pain was disappointing and causing more anxiety and anguish. At one point I grabbed my husband by the collar and asked him to tell them to stop this process and that I'll come back tomorrow.

He frantically said with sadness in his eyes, "You know we can't do that." He was hugging and rubbing my head. Nothing was consoling. The pains were so frequent, I could hardly catch my breath between contractions.

The nurse appeared and examined me again. She decided to prepare me for an Epidural and asked that I not push down because the baby is in the delivery position. The doctor appeared dressed for the procedure. They had me lie on my side with my knees to my chest. I wondered how that was possible with a baby in between. I did my best. I felt cold liquid spray on my back and a deep tug within my spine. Within minutes an anesthetic was administered. I was then turned to lie flat on my back, and my feet placed in the stirrups.

The doctor was positioned on a rolling seat between my legs and my husband positioned himself, directly behind the doctors' head.

I was asked to push as hard as I could and then asked abruptly to stop. The baby's head was putting pressure on the vaginal opening. The doctor needed to cut the skin between my anus and vaginal opening to allow a greater opening. By now I was completely numb from the waist down and felt nothing.

My husband yelled "Jenny, your ass just broke." I looked at him with disgust as he said this awful thing. The doctor remarked the pressure had caused a small hemorrhoid. My senses heightened as I became aware that I was having a baby.

Minutes later our baby was born. "Jenny it's a boy!" said my husband.

I didn't hear any crying. The nurse carried him to the warming bassinet, where I could turn my head to see her examine him. My husband stood next to her with a big smile on his face. As she rubbed his tiny body with a towel, he began to whimper. She swaddled him in a blanket and continued her examination. He was six pounds four ounces and 18 inches long.

There were early signs that we had a high functioning child. The nurse asked us to watch her, as she applied a tiny oxygen mask to our baby's face, and he raised his tiny hands and attempted to push away the apparatus. We were both amazed and bewildered. The nurse replied, "I've never seen a newborn exhibit motor skill like this before."

On the second day at the hospital, my husband sat near me on a chair holding our newborn, sobbing uncontrollably. Between the sobs he asked that I never take his son away from him, which I agreed never to do. I realized how saddened he had been over not being able to see the two boys he fathered with his last girlfriend.

She restricted him to two to three times a year, if any. Trying to communicate with her was nearly impossible.

I also understood his ex-girlfriend's emotional pain. He would abandon her to her mother with two-week-old and two-year-old sons. I want to believe he loved her as much as she loved him. There was deception between them concerning their expectations for their relationship. Considering all of this, I said again, "I will never take your son away from you and that is a promise." He smiled through his tears.

A month before I went into labor, JC's older son spent the summer with us. He was eight years old at the time. JC spoke with his ex-girlfriend, explaining he wanted all of his boys to be together for a day. She agreed to let him take their two boys. He brought them back to our house. I watched in amazement at how the older boy interacted with his younger brothers as though they already knew each other. This gave me the opportunity to observe him interacting with all of his boys and found him to be loving, playful, sympathetic, and warmhearted with them. He looked like the perfect father.

Upon being discharged from the hospital, my husband ran around town to pick up a car seat. He arrived with flowers as well and a great big smile. The occasion was festive, but I felt lonely, confused, and depressed. I had no idea how to care for a baby. When we arrived home, I walked in and laid the baby in the middle of the bed.

I folded my arms and asked, "What am I to do with this baby?" I began to cry.

He hugged me saying, "It's going to be okay. I know you are afraid, but I know enough to teach you what to do."

During the next six weeks, my husband was truly a great father; he took on all the night feeding duties so I should get rest. There were many nights the baby did not sleep, so I got no sleep. My husband asked to take the baby to his parents for 24 hours so I could sleep. I agreed. During this time, I realized I was struggling with post-partum depression. I missed him and the baby, the first eight hours they were gone and began to worry about the baby. I felt crazy, of course the baby was okay, still I placed a phone call just for assurance.

We were soon back to work, and my in-laws were happy to babysit. We realized our small home was strangely even smaller. We were able to move into a larger one to raise our son who was then three-month-old. My husband was extremely possessive of our son; I knew it was because he was truly grateful to have him. He still insisted on doing night duty, which I was happy to have him do.

My depression subsided and I was beginning to feel like a mother. Watching him play with toys with his feet and try holding his bottle was fun. I became fascinated with his presence. I began to learn if he was crying because he was wet, hungry, or wanted to be picked up.

I played classical music after work, which set the tone in a peaceful manner during the evening. Our relationship flourished and we returned to our love for eating out. Once we left the baby bottle at home by mistake and took turns walking around with him, while the other ate. We never made that mistake again. We still struggled with bills and getting better paying jobs. We had no idea how expensive it was to care for a child during the first year of life.

The day after Mothers' Day, my husband called saying I needed to go quickly to my in-laws and pick up the baby. Something had happened to his mother. The paramedics were there when I arrived. My father-in-law was coming out with the baby in one arm and his wife's purse in the other. My husband soon arrived. We were all nervous and pushed the paramedics for information.

I wondered if she had already passed away, because they did not leave for about 20 minutes.

Soon we were instructed to meet them at the hospital. We rode together. My husband questioned his stepfather on the details leading up to the 911 call. He replied they all had just finished eating and she complained of chest pain. He thought it was angina and went to get her medication from the bathroom. When he walked back into the room, she had slumped over in her chair.

We got to the hospital and were taken to a family waiting room. It seemed like eons before we got the news. She had passed away. I was holding the baby who was now nine months old and able to crawl. I put him on the floor and went over to console my husband and father-in-law. We were all crying. The doctor said she had an enlarged heart and there was nothing they could do to save her.

When we began to calm down, we looked for the baby, who was now walking around in the room. I gasped for air, saying, "Oh my God, how is it that a nine-month-old child can walk?"

My husband still shaken said, "It's my mother's spirit that has gone into her grandson." I looked on, horrified.

My father-in-law said, "We have noticed him crawling on one knee and pulling himself to stand using the furniture." Watching this small child walk un-aided was a miracle.

Three months later we were planning our son's first birthday party with excitement. We were able to have JC's oldest son visit again. The last time we saw him, I was pregnant in my last trimester. When he and his dad arrived, we had moved into a bigger house. He came inside and gazed at our son.

He said, "Wow the last time I was here, he wasn't born yet, and he is walking around?"

JC responded, "Yeah, we are also amazed. He started walking at nine months old. We never really watched him crawl. He would sort of scoot with one knee."

His son laughed, "I didn't know babies could walk so early, he is so little."

I watched the interaction between the two flourish into brotherhood.

Our toddler was walking and able to climb in and out of his crib. He went into his room and brought his toys to play. What was unfolding was amazing.

My stepson had a nickname, "Bubba". Our son learned how to pronounce the name and one morning as Bubba slept, I witnessed our toddler go into his brothers' room. He walked over to the bed while Bubba was still asleep. He began to pat him on the shoulder, and called, "Bu- Ba" several times. His brother rolled over with a big smile.

I said, "He talks too."

The day came to celebrate our son's first birthday. The atmosphere was exciting. Family and friends arrived with their children and gifts. My son's godmother brought the cake. Daddy was putting up decorations, as my toddler was moving about the house as usual. A few more guests were arriving with more food and gifts. I was harried in the kitchen putting the food trays together.

I heard a faint cry, "Oh my God, he has a cockroach wing on his face!" screamed one of our guests. I bolted from the kitchen to see what was happening and witnessed my son with part of an insect wing on his cheek.

I was horrified as I grabbed him and placed him on my lap. I asked, "What have you been eating?" He looked at me with a smile. I then pried his mouth open to look around but found nothing.

My coworker said, "Well, if he ate the roach, it's great protein."

I was not amused! But everyone else burst into laughter. Another family member snapped a picture of the wing pasted on the side of his mouth. That picture still sits on the coffee table in my home.

CHAPTER 10

Re-directed

When our son was 15 months old, my husband decided we should move back to Miami; so, he contacted a friend inquiring about work. His friend was helping to spearhead some drug treatment programs and needed staff. A position was offered to my husband and soon we were packed and headed South. My mother agreed to let us live with her.

As my mother got to interact with her grandson, she spoke about her amazement in his language skills. She told us of an incident where she had passed gas. Our son said, "Gamma, you make poo poo? Lay down let me change your diaper."

She laughed and thought he spoke better than any toddler she had ever interreacted with, meaning her other three grandchildren. She thought he was too high functioning, so I asked her what we should do. She suggested we have him evaluated at the Child Development Center at the University of Miami. My husband and I gave her the okay to set up an appointment.

By the time his appointment was set, our son was 20 months old and running. He was fully communicative and made complete sentences. One day I picked him up from daycare, as we were headed to the car I asked, "How was your day?" He reported his daycare teacher put tape over his mouth. I abruptly made a u-turn back into the building and spoke privately with the teacher. I let her know that what she did was child abuse, and I could file a complaint. She didn't deny it, but explained her reason was that he talks a lot. Attempting to smooth it over, she then said, "I was playing with him." I said to her, "See how much talking he is capable of? He told on you." I agreed not to open a case, as long as she never did that again, not just to my child but any child.

Within the next six months we both graduated, I as a licensed practical nurse and my husband with a degree in Human Resource Management. He got a new position with Miami Dade County; division of the court system and I went to work at the hospital where I was born, Mount Sinai.

As our lives got busier, I felt a change in our relationship. My husband did not want to socialize much anymore. He was okay with me going out with my mother or women friends he knew. He monitored and asked multiple questions about where my mother or any other friend invited us. He was paranoid and made negative comments about people in situations that he did not know. He was always on guard, as though he believed something was going to happen. I was not able to mentally figure out what his motives were. I did come to believe he was anti-social.

Still some physical domestic violence occurred infrequently, but the emotional abuse was worse. He told me that I would no longer be able to make financial decisions about anything, because I was poor at taking care of finances. A time came when the inside component of our central AC stopped working in the summer.

I asked a coworker, whose father owned an AC company, if her father could help us. I explained the problem and she reiterated it to her dad.

He said he had a unit and would sell and install the part for 300 dollars. I was so excited. When he arrived home, I shared the news. He grew angry and told me; I was not allowed to conduct any household business and I had better stay in my place or he would have to resort to other means. I was so frightened from the past physical abuse, I said nothing.

As our son grew older, at around three years old, his behavior was no better. He was diagnosed with Attention Deficit Hyperactivity Disorder (ADHD). He was always on the move. He wasn't violent but always ran around and would not sit down. His vocabulary was more advanced. He would converse with other children during times when he should be quiet. He refused to stay in his cot during nap time, which his daycare teacher complained of. He did not have the ability to pay attention.

We were constantly being called from the daycare about his in-ability to stay focused and interact with the other kids appropriately. This took a toll on the marriage. One day I received a call from the daycare, to come and pick up our child because he was being expelled. At three? I thought how absurd.

We searched for another daycare and found Beacon Hill school. We got an appointment with the headmaster and explained our dilemma. The woman was so kind and understanding. She said they actually had other children with the same disorder and would be happy to have him come there for a more one-on-one type of education approach. It all sounded great, but there was a massive cost and how would it fit in our budget.

This became an emotional problem for us both. We decided we would have to cut costs somehow, even if it meant not eating out, not buying any new clothing and definitely no short getaways. Our son's future was at stake.

At his new school, his first teacher was an elderly Jamaican lady who had taught young children for many years. She was stern, unkind, and put him in time out often for speaking. She reported to us on many occasions that our son was deviant and hardheaded. She was trying to crack him from this incessant talking. She said he struggled to stay focused, even in a small classroom setting, but his verbal skills were far beyond his chronological age and were actually impeccable.

We reported these observations to the principal, who decided to change teachers to give our son more opportunities to use his verbal skills in a strategic manner. He was given tasks such as reading to the class, making short announcements of what the class schedule was to be for the day, this was their strategy for use of his high energy, in an attempt to teach him.

By the age of five, he continued to have verbal outbursts and found it difficult to stay on task. Many evenings we sat up with him doing simple homework. If our dog came near or ran under the table, our son's attention went to the dog. It became difficult to re-direct his attention.

We decided to seek help from a child psychologist. After a couple of years of sessions, the psychologist suggested that he be placed on medication, because his behavior was not getting much better. My husband was totally against the idea. He thought of how his parents allowed the medical establishment to put him on drugs, which were for adults and those drugs nearly killed him. I explained, I know his fears, but the medicines were safer for children and we, along with the psychologist, could monitor our son's progress.

Still, I relented about starting medication for fear of physical and emotional retaliation. The psychologist continued to work with us, explaining we were to engage our son in as many extra-curricular activities as possible to get him to calm down. We signed him up for everything imaginable; dance class, little league sports, daily down time to listen to classical music and part time piano lessons.

It became more chores for our son, on top of our busy work schedules. Our relationship deteriorated even more. We argued about how to discipline, hand down consequences and keep the constant schedules we had for all three of us. I felt depressed. The communication between us was nearly nonexistent. He was just as agitated about our plight. There was less sex and less emotional support.

I asked my husband if he would be okay with the two of us attending marriage counseling. He turned and yelled, "I don't need any type of counseling, I am a psychologist," And he walked away.

Soon we both progressed more in our jobs with better positions and pay. My husband was instrumental in getting our son into two dance schools, as well as finding him a talent agent who specialized in getting acting and print roles for children.

Upon the talent agent meeting our son for the first time, she thought he was extremely intelligent and asked us to allow her to put him under contract. My husband was ecstatic and said yes. I had reservations because this could add to the already hectic schedules, we all had. I asked for time to think it over, which she accepted. After careful examination of our schedules and duties, we were able to reschedule some of the activities our son had not excelled at, and my husband agreed to run our son around on the weekends to whatever programs we decided to keep.

I was allowed to take the Saturdays to clean, attend to laundry, cook, and handle all other chores I missed during the week. Of course, there were recitals that we both had to attend on the weekends. I became content with my son responding to the life activities he was excited to do. For the first time in a while, I saw us come together as a couple with a special child who might respond to even more activity.

His agent was able to get him quite a few low paying print and local television advertisement jobs. Our son seemed to love that, and his hyperactive behavior was less when he was doing these activities. We were both amazed.

As our son entered middle school in the local school system, we started to recognize his ability to play keyboard and sing. He had excelled in the dance of ballet, modern, jazz and tap dance. He appeared more comfortable about his ability to manage his thoughts and verbal outbursts minimized.

But then I received a call from the school counselor, that our son had been in physical confrontation with another student, and we should come to the school as soon as possible. I called my husband and asked that we meet at the school. When we arrived, our son was in the counselor's office. She reported our son was struck in the face by a female student, following an argument. He retaliated by throwing a desk at her. They both were suspended for one week. My husband and I were shocked. We explained that our son was always very talkative, but never physically violent. Our suspicion was the change from private school to public school may have triggered this aggression.

We had a new dilemma. When we arrived at home, we sat down to hash out our son's feelings about changing schools. He said, "The students are not like the students at my other school. They are unruly and they don't pay attention in the classroom." Paper and bubblegum wads had been thrown at him several times. The girl he had the altercation with was mean and nasty from the first day of school. "I hate this new school, and I don't want to go back."

He started to cry. His father consoled him and let him know we would see if he could go back to his private school. The following day, we requested a meeting with the director of the private school. We explained the situation and she thought it would be a great idea and told us they would love to have him back.

CHAPTER 11

Additions to Our Family

One Sunday the phone rang; I was in another part of the house working on a report and did not know who was calling. A couple of minutes later, my husband entered the room and said we had to get to Saint Petersburg, Fl right away. His 12-year-old son, from the relationship with the woman he never married, called, and asked to come live with us. His mother had married a man and in that relationship her drug use increased. He said there were many mornings that he and his two younger sisters were never awakened in time to prepare to go to school, so the responsibility had fallen on him.

He told his dad that he didn't get along with his stepfather at all, and he didn't want to live there anymore. He begged him to come and rescue him.

I comforted my husband and said, "We are an intact family inclusive of all your children. Remember what I told you just before we got married, marrying you means I marry you and your children." I asked him to give me a few minutes to grab our son and get some snacks and activities for the ride.

As we traveled, I had all sorts of memories of the many times we sent money and gifts to the children, only to have them returned. My husband cried each time it happened. He vowed things would get better one day. At least he had our son and his first born in his life.

When the boys were five and seven years old, their mother contacted my husband after four years of estrangement. She asked to have the children put on his insurance. She said Medicaid was tightening her case and forcing her to get a job. She had been unsuccessful to date and wanted them insured. My husband agreed with her. He was happy that he could have some influence in their lives.

She said she had two more children, daughters and was in a relationship with their father. After this insurance agreement, the boys were allowed telephone contact with their father. My husband and son had traveled to see the boys a few times over the last 6 years.

When we arrived at the home in Saint Pete, we found my husband's son sitting on the front porch with a duffle bag and a large TV box, which contained his belongings. He looked sad and began to cry as his father embraced him. My husband inquired as to the whereabouts of his mother. To which his son replied, "They all went out to shop, and he was home alone."

His mother was upset that he chose to leave and threw his belongings in the box. She said, "I won't be here when your dad arrives, I don't want to see them."

His son said he hoped his brother would look after his two sisters, but he didn't want to be there anymore. We quickly gathered his things and headed back to Miami.

I was in school at this time and working part time. I wondered how we were going to manage. Soon after my stepson settled into his new home, at the age of 40 and about to enter my last year of nursing school, I was diagnosed with breast cancer. The news came as a shock. I was in a step aerobics class and as we were cooling down, I rubbed an area of my left breast and felt a lump. When I got home, I discussed my findings with my husband, and he felt the lump as well. I saw my primary care doctor as soon as possible and he subsequently ordered a mammogram. It turned out I required surgery and needed to find an oncologist.

I discussed this issue with my anatomy and physiology professor, who was also a medical doctor, and asked if he could recommend an oncologist. He was quiet for a few moments and finally said, "I'm so sorry for your trouble, especially in this last fall semester before registered nurse(RN) school." He then scratched his head, as if in quiet contemplation. He said, "If you were my wife or daughter, I would recommend the Sylvester Cancer Center at the University of Miami." I thanked him.

I was evaluated at the cancer center and advised to have surgery to only remove a small lump. Chemotherapy was recommended as a precaution to prevent the cancer from spreading.

The fear for my life loomed large. I had so many irons in the fire. I was in school full time, working part time and caring for my family. I wondered how to get it all done without dropping out of college. I confided in a classmate, and she said, "Girl we are getting old and trying to further our education, just let them cut off the titty and we can keep on rolling." I looked at her and burst into laughter with tears. I could not imagine how she could say something so awful, but I understood the reason. I needed to keep going no matter what because my goal was to be an RN.

I had surgery and managed to miss only 3 days of classes. I agreed to start chemotherapy after the semester ended.

I was carded to start RN classes in the winter and decided to get chemotherapy on the days I was not in class. My husband advised, "I should be cautious and speak to the dean, to make them aware of my current condition." I agreed. I had this discussion with the dean of the school before classes began.

She said, "Chemotherapy is tough and sickening and perhaps you should consider starting the program next year."

I responded, "I'm 40 years old and being an RN is my ultimate goal. The fact that my good grades and acceptance to this program gave me assurance of graduating. I choose to press on, and if the time comes that I'm too sick to carry on, I will let you know."

She said I would be allowed to miss three days each semester and she gave me her okay to go on.

My husband and the boys were afraid for me. The boys thought the word cancer meant certain death. I explained the surgical procedure and shared that chemotherapy was just a precaution. My husband and I assured them that I would be alright. They helped to keep the house clean and were instrumental in preparing meals. They kept up with after school schedules and events and comforted me often with kisses and hugs. Each time my stepson told me he loved me just warmed my heart. I felt his fear for me.

My husband said, "I know you are having a tough time, but at least you are alive, and I expect you will come through all of this valiantly."

I completed the one-year program, while being sick as a dog on chemo days, but I was determined to not give up or give in. I was honored when I was asked to give a speech at my class graduation on how I got through school.

By graduation I had finished chemotherapy. I was healthy and back to being a mother. I continued to work part time and began studying for the state board exam.

CHAPTER 12

Marching Onward

Because I had been successful in pulling through my illness and graduating college, I began to feel the need to find a church to worship. Nearly all of my adult life I had been un-churched. My experience of church consisted of a minister in the pulpit yelling Bible verses, that I was unable to understand and saw no significant improvement in my life by attending. I felt a desire to know the higher source, because of the health issue I passed through. If anything had happened and I passed away, I would not know God. I recruited my mom to visit local churches with me on Sundays. She agreed. We visited several churches all over Miami, over a six-week period, but the messages did not seem relevant to what I was seeking.

One Sunday when I picked up Mom, and I told her we would start visiting churches, right in the neighborhood where I had grown up, the very northern end of Miami Dade County. I was not impressed with the churches in our new search area. I was seeking more life altering, thought provoking sermons.

However, one Sunday I pulled into the parking lot of a church called Universal Truth Center. I'm amazed that I can still remember the sermon the Late Rev. Doctor Mary A Tumpkin preached. It was the Sunday before the 1998 Martin Luther King Holiday.

The lesson sermon, as they so lovingly call them was titled "Where Does Peace Begin?" Rev. Tumpkin spoke about the peace we don't feel for ourselves, or spouses or significant others, our children, neighbors, family, co-workers, or the world in which we live. She preached that peace must begin within. I had never been to a church that delivers practical information to live by. She would lovingly say, "When you come into this church, bring your brains with you; because there is much to learn about yourself."

After that first service, we were shown around the facility by one of the members, and everyone - total strangers- shook hands or offered hugs. It felt good, loving, and inviting.

Prior to going inside of the church that day, my mother made it clear that I knew that the people in the community said the church was a cult. I politely said, "Mom, with all of the fights for my life that I have before me, no cult could sway me to do anything, that I thought was not good for me and in my best interest."

After the service as we headed to the car, my mom said, "Well if this church is brain washing people, then I want my brain washed, dried and folded." We laughed all the way home.

On our next visit, I was convinced that I should join that teaching center. My mother sanctioned my decision and went to church with me over the next 10 years, until she was diagnosed with Alzheimer's disease and could go no more.

Over the next three years, I delved deep into the "Better Living" weekly classes and Sunday services. I volunteered with the Time Tithers Committee for whatever was needed. I began to feel that my life had purpose, but in actuality; I had been very depressed 20 years before I walked in their doors.

I began to feel alive as I took this "New Thought" teaching to task. I started meditating two to three times a day, five to fifteen minutes at a time. I read the book - "Lessons in Truth" by H. Emily Cady. I invited my family to attend. My husband and the boys went one time, but my stepson desired to go more often.

One Sunday as the services had ended, he said he wanted to ask me a few questions. He asked, "Why did my mom say so many terrible things about you?" He stated, "I've been living with you and dad for a year, and all of the bad things my mom said about you are not true." You have treated me as your own son and have never shown anything but love."

I explained that when people feel hurt, betrayed, or let down by another person, especially someone they have children with and or are married to, they only know to say mean things to hurt others, because they feel so hurt.

"Your mother was simply showing these emotions and you and your older brother were experiencing them. This is how hurt people react to their pain and hurt. I don't think she had any intention of telling lies about me. She was acting out of her anger and frustration."

My husband was a great singer with an operatic voice. When I first met him at work, he was always singing. He even attempted to create a singing group with his employees. It never panned out. He hit false eta's as well as bass tones with ease. He said "Pursuing a singing career was what he wished for most of his life, but being a parent left no room for that.

One day our son's talent agent notified us that she wanted him to travel to Orlando to audition for a TV series for children called, "Gulla Gulla Island". He needed to be brought there for at least a week. I asked my mother, since she was retired, to take on this task and she did. They were placed in a hotel with all meals. My son was assigned a tutor, and my mom would be the chaperone. We were all excited for him, as he nailed the audition and got the part.

He was professional and detailed in his role, according to my mother, and he played his role with all his heart. He was not bothered by the hundreds of words in the script, or the times the director yelled, "Cut!" Friends and family would tell me they saw the one episode on TV. We were given the final cut on VHS.

My husband discussed expanding his son's talent by purchasing a keyboard. He himself was also musically talented with a beautiful singing voice. He and I discussed that one day he would dive into a singing career, but marriage, children, and careers clouded this dream.

He introduced the keyboard and soon he and the boys could not get enough of it. They were exploring the different sounds, keystrokes, and the music writing capability of the keyboard. It produced every musical instrument with beats and bops.

There was a lot of discussion on turning poems into music with both of his sons. They worked on that idea daily.

In my son's ninth grade school year, he played the lead role in "Oklahoma". As I watched his performance, I was amazed at how well he sang and performed the entire show. His singing was impeccable. He hit notes I had never heard him practice. My best friend attended with me. At the close of the show, my son received a standing ovation.

My friend asked, "Where is his bouquet of flowers?"

I responded, "I've heard him singing around the house, but I did not know he had that level capability of carrying and singing an entire play." He would be a star one day.

CHAPTER 13

Set Back

As I continued practicing and living by the principles taught by the loving community of Universal Truth Center, I was diagnosed with a recurrence of cancer. My physicians wanted me to go on chemotherapy again as well as radiation.

I started chemotherapy first with plans to then begin radiation. My body did not react very well after the first dose of chemotherapy. As the infusion started, I began to experience burning along my gastrointestinal tract. The burning went from my mouth to my anus and sent me to the bathroom with horrible diarrhea and stomach pain.

After that first high dose, I found myself near death with little to no white blood cells. I was weak, listless and ran a high fever. I notified my doctor, and she suggested I come to the hospital as soon as possible, so I could be in a protective environment. I was placed in an isolation room, to protect me, while in the hospital. The chemotherapy was halted until I could gain more white blood cells. This frightened me, but I believed I could get through anything with the power of positive thinking. I let my doctor know I would be seeking a second opinion before moving through the next three doses. She said I was entitled to do that. I quickly found a doctor at Baptist Healthcare system. He examined me and looked at my records.

His recommendation was that I could get through the next three doses if the medicine doses were lessened according to a lower body weight as opposed to my weight at the time. He said he had used this method before, when patients experienced severe side effects from one dose. This information was sent to my primary oncologist, and she agreed to follow what the second opinion was.

The next six months took a toll on my marriage and my boys. They were reliving another cancer diagnosis all over again. I saw fear in my husband, as I entertained that fear as well. I thought a lot about how unhappy I had become in the marriage over the years. Simply trying to take care of myself was exacerbating. I thought for sure that if I remained in the marriage, it would kill me, and my husband would be off marrying someone else. After all, I desired to be out of the marriage after the first year. Now my health was at stake.

I continued to go to church and take Better Living Classes, and one day I shared my cancer re-occurrence with my minister. She asked to pray with me, and I agreed. While in her office in silence she asked to sit before me holding hands. I closed my eyes as she did, and she began to pray. Soon tears were flowing from my eyes. When she finished her prayer, she said, "You don't have a health problem, you have a forgiveness problem." She said, "Breast cancer comes from deep hurt and resentment." The tears flowed more, as I began to sob. She was right. All these years I resented my father, stepfather, Mom's third husband, and my husband. They all had hurt me in different ways.

My father never wanted to visit with or see my brother and I for years, my stepfather physically abused us all and my husband had been physically, mentally, and emotionally abusive to me for years.

I continued to pray, journal, especially about the truth of my physical and emotional thoughts, go to church services, and meditate through these obstacles. Also, I continued with my macrobiotic diet, eliminating meat, except fish.

I managed to finish the high dose chemotherapy and radiation and have been cancer free.

CHAPTER 14

Lived Experiences

I took a class at church one semester taught by the Rev Dr. Anna Price. She announced there would be a term paper requested at the end of the semester. She had suggestions for the term paper written on small, folded pieces of paper. She placed them in a hat, passed the hat around for us to choose our topic.

My question read: "Can anything manifest in your life, world and affairs, which had not come from the subconscious phase of mind?" That meant to me, if I think about it, I bring the idea forward. A man is as he thinks. WOW. I soon began to ponder how I would write a paper based on this question. The next day it came to me that everything that had occurred in my marriage was based on thoughts and feelings stored in my subconscious mind.

I thought back to the very day, a year after I was married, when my mother called to wish me a happy first year anniversary; and I told her I had made a mistake.

I then realized I had dropped this unhappiness into my subconscious mind, and it single-handedly worked itself into my life, world, and affairs. All the arguments, discourse, jealousy, rage, anger, physical abuse, domestic violence, mental and emotional abuse, I had experienced was all set-in motion by me, because I did not want marriage anymore.

As I wrote that four-page term paper, I realized that the question was for my release from the bondage I had put myself in all those years. I also realized I had given away all my power, for so called love. I saw this term paper as my ticket out, no matter what I had endured all these 20 years. I asked my husband one Sunday to take a ride with me, I wanted to talk to him. I let him know I did not want to be in the marriage anymore and that I was leaving. He said in a threatening manner, that I needed to stay until our son graduated from high school. I knew that could not happen. If I stayed in that marriage, I would surely perish.

My son asked his father one day if his coworker would plait his hair, he wanted the twisted hair to become dreadlocks. He sounded as though he knew and had a relationship with this person already. I asked my husband, "Who is this person?"

He said, "It's just my coworker who is also a hair stylist.

I asked, "Where is her salon?"

He replied, "She does hair styles at her home."

He gave me a location but not an address and only her initials. I replied, "How is it I've never heard mention of this person before now?"

He adamantly explained that she is just a coworker who likes to write poetry. He read some of her work and introduced her to our son so they might be able to collaborate on putting her work into songs. Our son was quite capable of doing that, so I had no more thoughts about this woman.

My husband soon asked if I would consider taking out a second mortgage, to start a small record label. I refused, reminding him that the boys would soon be looking to go to college, and we were not yet prepared for that. Perhaps a second mortgage might be needed for their education. He argued, attempting to show me how a record deal could produce considerable income.

I stated, "This idea is your dream, not mine or the boys and the timing is not right."

He stated, "I've done any and everything that you've asked me to do over the years and I ask for one thing, and you refuse? You'll see how this turns out!" He stormed out of the room.

In an instant, he stopped communicating with me about everything, except our budget and the boys. The next year of marriage became worse. Although we lived in the same home and paid the necessary bills, and took care of the boys, he refused to talk to me or socialize with me or my family. I would ask him how his day was, and he would nod and walk out. He stopped sleeping in our bed, so no sex. I felt his cold-hearted behavior. He went as far as to stop going on summer vacation with us. His excuse was he needed to save money for his own record label. I thought he would snap out of that behavior and tried to speak with him in a loving manner when we were alone. He looked at me with disdain.

I could see the boys were looking at us strangely, but they never asked any questions. My stepson was headed into his senior year and spent a lot of time with friends and his girlfriend. He was in the school choir and participated in drama and performances.

My son was in senior high in ninth grade. He still participated in auditions; his agent would send as well as the drama department.

They managed the situation by letting us know their needs. A ride to and from school or to a friend's house was being done by us both.

The house was busy, and I didn't make a lot of noise about the situation. I remembered how volatile he could be and wanted none of that to occur if I could help it. I was simply afraid of him.

Toward the end of my stepson's senior year, he decided to move in with a classmate. We spoke about his reasoning for this decision. He explained that it was too much anger and frustration living with us and since he spent a lot of time with his classmates, his parents agreed to let him come stay with them. My husband and I met and spoke with the parents of the classmate. They had a lovely home and one son. They said they enjoyed having our son stay over, that he was quiet, polite, and enjoyable. Their son loved their relationship. Our stepson would soon be graduating from high school and had plans to move to a neighboring county to practice horticulture. We all sanctioned the decisions.

One Saturday, my husband came home with a tuxedo across his back. I asked as he entered the door, "Oh, wow, where are we going?"

He replied, "You and I are going nowhere." He proceeded down the hall, took a shower, got dressed in that beautiful black tuxedo and left.

I felt saddened and unloved. All of the previous times we had gone to the Kappa balls and New Year Eve's parties, several cruises, and all required evening wear.

It felt good for a second to remember the last 10 years of our fun times. I had thoughts that he was all dressed up because he was having an affair, or had a set of friends I knew nothing about or maybe he was attending a work affair? It felt horrible not to know anything for the first time in our relationship. I felt like an outsider.

My son witnessed the behavior of his father and asked why I looked so sad.

I sat him down and let him know that I would be leaving his father, but that I needed time to prepare. I wanted him to remain in our family home with his dad. I stated that when he was born, his teary-eyed father asked me to never take his son away from him, as the women of his last relationships had done.

I let him know I loved his father, but we just did not get along anymore, and it was in my best interest to move out. I let him know that I would not be going far, but to a place near his school and that I would still pick him up daily and he could come on the weekend and spend time with me. I told him that his father needed him, and he agreed.

I began looking at all of my options, emotionally and financially. I decided to take this idea to heart and not rush it.

I began to feel another shift in my awareness about my relationship with my husband. I thought, *"I could have been dead and gone from the cancer, and this guy would be with someone else."* Perhaps he was already seeing another woman.

He was spending a lot of time being away at night. He said he had found a music studio to possibly record some of the music he and our sons had written. It seemed odd that he would be doing this into the wee hours of the morning.

I decided to check out the area where the coworker/hair stylist lived. I drove to the vicinity and found a cluster of four-story apartments. I drove in and out of each parking row looking for his car. As I rounded the last row, I saw his car. There was a space next to it, so I backed in. If I had known the apartment number, I would have approached it and rang the doorbell. This was the place he had been coming and staying half the night. He had to come out of one of these apartments soon, I reasoned. I decided to wait.

As I waited, I broke down crying and began to scream and hit the steering wheel. The anger was so palpable, I thought if I saw him then, I would attack him. The thought of hurting someone else scared me. I felt weak all over and it was hard to gain my composure.

As I continued to wait, I called my sister-in-law who was newly divorced from my brother. I told her where I was and what the situation was. I spoke about the despair I was feeling.

She said, "Remember when your brother and I split up? You told me anyone that does not want or love you anymore, you can't continue to want nor to love them. Go home." She also shared, "Because of your fragile state of health, just finishing chemotherapy, perhaps you should concentrate on your health and get out of your bad marriage. If not, the cancer could come back and kill you from the stress."

I thanked her for the wisdom, ended the call, exited my car, went to my husband's car, and placed a note on the seat. It read, "You're a liar! You are supposed to be at a studio, does not look like a studio area to me." I locked his car and drove home.

I went to bed as it was quite late. Around three a.m., I was awakened by the sound of him entering the house. I heard him walking down the hallway toward our room. I had the bedroom door closed but not locked.

As he opened the door, he said "What is this note you placed in my car about?"

I replied, "I have to work in the morning and I'm not going to discuss it. You can go and sleep somewhere else, oh and please close the door behind you."

The next day was as usual, he did not talk to me. I had nothing to say to him.

The time had come. I needed to break away from this failing marriage. I wished to have my freedom and life back.

Over the following weeks, I prepared myself mentally for single life again. I made it clear to my son that I would be the same mother, doing the same things for him, even though I would not be living there, as promised.

I considered moving back home, but felt I needed time alone to sort out my life. My mother had been diagnosed with dementia but was still able to take care of herself. We spoke daily and I could tell by her tone, she was not happy with me leaving the marriage. The last thing I wanted was to bring my drama to her home. She continued to have a good relationship with my husband. He had always thought of her as a mother figure.

I found a one-bedroom apartment near my son's school. I announced one Saturday morning that I was moving out and he, my husband, said sarcastically, "Do you want some help?"

I replied, "Sure. Thanks."

Since we owned a truck, it seemed feasible to use what was already available. He agreed, but I saw exacerbation written all over his face. Me, my son, and husband grabbed items within the house that I wanted, loaded them onto our pickup truck and off we went to an apartment complex. I had already picked up the keys the day before and remembered when I put the key in the keyhole, turned the knob and opened the door, I began to sob and fell to my knees. It played out in my mind in slow motion.

I cried because I had my freedom back, which I thought would never be possible. I cried because I had left my lovely home for a one-bedroom apartment, I cried because God had given me the courage to step into uncharted waters with only $535 in my pocket and insurmountable personal and spousal debt.

Surely, I felt blessed; I felt that the high blood pressure I had carried since age 30 would go away. I felt I would never have another terrible diagnosis again, because I had learned the principles of God and did not ever have to be a victim. I found myself and freedom again being single. I took a lot of debt with me and wondered from paycheck to paycheck how I would pay two car notes, the second mortgage as well as my rent and all the credit card debt I was in. I stopped worrying and placed my trust in God.

Three months into single life, my ex-husband called to say my mother was not doing well. Although she had been diagnosed with dementia two years before, I found her to be very functional. He said he went to visit and found her disheveled and thinner. He said he sat down to chat with her and later asked for a glass of water. She invited him to go ahead to the kitchen and help himself. He reported that he suspected my mother was not eating, because there was little to no food in the refrigerator, but there were quite a few bottles of liquor.

He then said sarcastically, that I should have moved home instead of moving into that apartment. I had no comment, other than to say I was too saddened having to leave my marriage, my son, and my spacious home for a one-bedroom apartment, to go home and care for my mother.

I let him know that I was dealing with my own level of stress after leaving our 20-year marriage and I did not have the energy to delve into my mom's illness. I did notice how she called and left several messages on the house phone daily. When I would call her before retiring to bed, she could not remember leaving the messages. She would always say she was doing fine and did not need my help.

I began to see how the breakup of my marriage and the demise of my brother's 25-year marriage could have changed my mother's mental capacity and aggravated her illness. My brother and I were her only two children.

I thought it would have been too hard for me. I lay awake many nights thinking about what he said, and one night just as I was dozing off, I heard a loud strong voice say, "Go Home." It scared me and I did not know what to make of it. I placed a call to my husband the next day and asked how I would be able to move home, when I had only been in the apartment 3 months and what about the security deposit?

He said to forget about the money, my mother needed someone to care for her and he would get a few friends together and move me to her home. He said he would do as much as he could to help me take care of her. He said, "As you know I'm fond of my mother-in-law."

Those few kind words and gestures brought this truth to me: my husband/friend of 38 years had always maintained relationships with his first mothers-in-law and his one girlfriend's mother. It's astonishing to me and I wondered if that was because he never knew his real mother.

Soon I moved into a small efficiency my mother had built some years prior behind her home; and this was great for me. My mother and I needed our own space.

My mom had not progressed into late stage of Alzheimer's, so I needed to hire someone to keep her company during the day and I was there at night. I was also able to travel, and my husband would make sure the daytime lady was there and our son could do night duty by simply spending the night. I noticed my mother would not turn on her own stove; I want to believe she knew she was losing her mind. So, all the cooking was done by others.

CHAPTER 15

The Uncovering

A few years before my mother's diagnosis, we all traveled to New York City and stayed with one of Mom's high school friends, Mrs. Margaret. She was long retired and was taking care of her spouse and was busy with community affairs. She treated us graciously and cooked three meals a day and insisted we eat.

A day before our flight back home, my mother announced that her diamonds and gold had been stolen. Mrs. Margaret as well as my husband and I looked bewildered. My mother had never left the house, but she had made mention before leaving Miami that New York was full of crime. We all looked feverishly for the jewelry but turned up nothing. Mrs. Margaret was most bewildered. We left for Miami without the jewelry.

A week later my mom received a UPS box that had her jewelry in it and a note that read, "Gladys I'm so sorry, but when I flipped the mattress on the bed you were sleeping in, I found your jewelry in a sock. I hope you are alright?"

I was shocked and could not figure out why my mother would hide her jewelry and not remember where she put it. Soon I was able to get a doctor's visit with a world-renowned physician, who specialized in Alzheimer's disease. After a battery of tests, Mom was diagnosed with early onset dementia, but I knew that at her age it could turn into Alzheimer's.

My brother and I were saddened for Mom, but we knew we had to decide how we would take care of her. I was able to get a job as a care manager working from home and seeing clients in the community as needed. This job was just what I needed to be able to manage Mom's care. JC continued to help me as much as he could.

We continued to co-parent our son. One day our son was going to Grad Night at Walt Disney World in Orlando, Florida, with the other high school seniors. He called and asked me to go to his house and pick up a jacket he forgot to pack. Since I was paying the mortgage on the house, I still had keys to it. I drove to the house and entered through the back door. I did not notice anything odd until I passed by my old bedroom and with a second look, thought I saw women's clothing and shoes. I retrieved the jacket and then proceeded into my bedroom, only to find my closet full of women's clothing and shoes. There was perfume, cosmetics, and jewelry all over the dresser. I was shocked.

I left quite upset. I wanted to call him and ask what was going on, but I was headed to the school to drop off the jacket for my son. I dared not get in an upsetting mood. When I got home, I called a friend to tell her what I had just seen. She asked if I had packed my suitcase yet.

I replied, "What does that have to do with what I had just told you?"

She replied, "We are traveling to California in the morning with the church." She said that I should drop the incident and pick it up when we got back home, and to focus on being happy about the trip. She was right.

While away, I had a phenomenal time but still could only think about why my husband disrespected me the way that he did. He had been kind and cordial during our separation, and I did not want to believe there was malice.

Upon returning home, I had concluded that he was merely trying to meet his needs, not hurt me in any way. I called him to request a meeting. He arrived after work. We sat down and I told him what I saw at the house. He lowered his head as though he was ashamed and said he only allowed the woman to come there as a housemate to offset his bills. I cried and he looked sadly, and said, "Jenny, I would never hurt you." I believed him.

CHAPTER 16

Easing into friendship

After we had been successfully separated for 2 years, my husband called and asked if I would grant him a divorce. I said I would have done it a while ago if he had been onboard with the idea. He confessed that he had fathered another child who was not expected to live, but she refused to die. He needed the divorce so she would not be bastardized.

I agreed to do whatever I could to help in the situation. We got the "Do it yourself divorce packet" and began filling out papers. We got a date to meet with a court mediator, who would go over the paperwork. There were about 100 pages. She asked about our son who was 17 at the time and said, if we waited until he turned 18 to make the divorce final, no one would have to pay court – mandated child support.

We agreed. However, she said with a do it yourself divorce, the court mandates that both parents and the child attend a three-hour mental health course at Miami Dade College. We took this to task and got an appointment for our son to attend his session in the morning on a Saturday, and we attend on the same day in the afternoon.

When we arrived at the location and entered the room, the instructor asked if we were together. We looked at each other and then the instructor before replying that we were together. Later at the onset of the class my husband asked the instructor why he had asked us if we were together. and he replied, "Because people getting divorced that have to take this class never show up together." We advised him that we didn't hate each other, and besides, we have a son whose wellbeing was important.

We had always maintained a level of civility for ourselves and our son. My husband once said, "We are educated people and if we act like fools because we are not together anymore, then what would our son see and how would he grow up? Should he not feel the love we have for him and once had for each other? Would he not know that we are still an intact family?"

The following year, I experienced shortness of breath, as I was finishing an aerobics class. I asked a friend to take me to the hospital. I had a diagnosis of mitral valve leakage. I was told to go home and get my affairs in order and be back to the hospital to prepare for surgery within 24 hours, or I risk losing my life.

I notified my employer, then I prepared my mother's nurse's aide to care for her more hours. I hired a private nursing company to be with her on the weekends. I did not know the turnaround time for my condition.

Prior to going into surgery, I was visited by Rev Lottie Clodfelter and Rev Charles Taylor for prayer, from my church, the Universal Truth Center. They were both staff ministers. I felt the Holy Spirit so strong just before entering the operating room. I felt as though I was floating. It was weird because I actually had no fear. I thought to myself, UTC *has me in mighty great prayer and I am alright*, and alright I was. Had I experienced anything like this in the past, it would have been terrifying, but it had to be done to save my life.

I did not want to upset my family, but I had to speak up, so someone would take care of Mom in my absence. I underwent surgery on a Friday and when I was released from the cardiac ICU, I was taken to a regular room, which was a small suite. Soon I was visited by my ex-husband and son. When they came into the room and saw the many tubes I was attached to, I knew they thought I was dying. I knew I was ok, just in a lot of pain. My ex-husband came to visit first upon me being released from the cardiac ICU. He let me know he had brought his new daughter named Amber Nicole and her mother, his new wife, with him. He said he was not permitted to bring the baby into my room and that she and the mother were in the patient visit area down the hall.

He came close, next to the bed and said he had gotten permission for me to take short walks within the room and he wanted to walk me to the door and back. It took considerable effort just to sit up on the side of the bed. To lift my head away from my chest was equally unbearable and painful because my breastbone had been sawed open.

I took my time with his assistance and eventually stood up. It was nauseating, and I thought I would collapse onto the floor. But I stood there for a minute as he had instructed and took some deep breaths. We then began to take slow steps toward the door. He spoke to me softly as though I was a child that he wanted to attend to. He assured me that I was doing a good job.

He encouraged me, "Try and lift your head just a little more, so you can see where you are going." As I did this, he gave me kudos again saying yes, see you can do it. He then said, "Okay, slowly, now let's turn around." I felt at that moment that he really loved and cared for me a great deal.

Before leaving my bedside, he asked if his daughter's mother could come and pray with me, while he attended to their daughter in the visitor's area. I agreed, because my ex-husband and I did not carry qualms about other relationships we had found ourselves in. We thought highly of ourselves as educated people. The fact that we were at one time madly in love with one another and that we had agreed to remain civil for our son's sake. We did not want him to grow up believing that his parents hated each other. The truth was that his parents loved each other but were not suited to be married anymore.

Three weeks later our son graduated high school and I was still unable to drive, so my ex-husband picked me up and we went to see our son graduate from high school, it was a beautiful thing. All our hard work had paid off. We soon went back to our separate lives with me in healing mode and him dealing with a child with disabilities.

My son had insisted on going to an out of state college and we never started a college fund all those years prior. Now we were faced with getting student loans for him.

Not long after, we found ourselves packing his things and accompanying him to college in

Connecticut. We all flew up together, rented a car and got his dorm room set up. It was bittersweet to see our baby going away from home, but we wanted what he wanted. We stayed over one night and headed back to Miami.

As we were leaving, my ex-husband asked, "Do you think we will hear from him soon?"

I replied, "I'm not sure but it may be a while. He more than likely feels free of our restrictions now."

CHAPTER 17

Connected at The Hip

Over the next couple of years, we went through the parents' kid going to college nightmare. Our son would call us both for money, he would not return phone calls, we were buying plane tickets for him to come home every holiday. These things on top of the cost of taking care of him on a regular basis.

One day my ex-husband asked how much money I was sending our son, because we both should not be sending so much money. He said we needed to communicate a little better with each other because he thought our son was taking advantage of us. Sure, enough he was, and we put a stop to it together.

Although we were not legally married anymore, we still operated like we were for our son's stability.

During his 2nd year in college, we got a call from the school saying that our son tried to harm himself by cutting his wrist. The school said that although he is an adult, they still had to notify us. We asked the school not to divulge that we were coming and flew out the next day. We got to the school and asked the registrar to call our son to the office without alerting him of our arrival. When he got to the office with a girl in tow, they both looked disheveled, and afraid.

We took him off campus and he insisted that his girlfriend accompany him. We acquiesced. We found a restaurant and sat down to figure out what happened.

Our son said they had a verbal altercation, and he became depressed because the relationship was called off. He wanted to hurt himself. He said they were now back together, and he would never attempt this again.

His father leaned in close to our son and said, "If you try anything like this again, you had better kill yourself without fail, or I will come here and do it for you!" He got the realness of the statement said to him. We flew home the next day.

CHAPTER 18

Time for travel

My ex-husband went on to take care of his new family and I commended him for having the willpower to care for his daughter and keep his other family going as well. He now had five children. The first with his initial wife, the second and third with a girlfriend, a forth with me and the fifth with his current wife. He was quite a lady's man.

All along he continued to help with anything or give advice I may need caring for my mom. He loved my mom as though she were his mother.

The year before my 50th birthday, I received a call from an old college friend living in Nigeria. He said, "Sis, what are you doing for your upcoming birthday? You will be turning the big 50!"

We spoke for a while about his life at home in Africa and his parents whom he was caring for. He said he had a place I could stay if I wanted to visit. I thought it was a wonderful idea. We agreed to do some travel homework for information on Visas and other pertinent information.

I asked my husband if he would tend to the financial aspects of Mom's care, i.e., paying the caregivers, reimbursement of petty cash and looking in on her every few days to make sure she was not being abused. He agreed. Soon I was off to Abuja, Nigeria with excitement and joy.

I flew from Miami international Airport to Amsterdam where there was a 6-hour layover. The airport was so large, I was astounded. There was a cathedral, bowling alley, casino, and a small shopping mall, under one roof. I boarded my second flight after being an airport tourist.

When I arrived and retrieved my luggage, I needed to get through customs. There was one lane open with approximately 50 people in front of me. I stood there praying and taking deep breaths. I've been out of the country before, but never experienced delays like that. I reached my friend to let him know I arrived safely. He told me it was rush hour and it would be an hour before he reached me. I found a place to sit and wait. When he arrived, he was driving a small car and had three men with him.

I thought, *"How is all of my luggage going to fit?"* We planned for me to be in Nigeria for 3 weeks. He quickly explained his car had broken down and he had to borrow his friend's car for transportation. I had a bad feeling about the situation.

We arrived at his home, which was a two-story building under re-construction. He and his friends removed my luggage and ushered me inside. I was introduced to his pregnant girlfriend and shown to my sleeping quarters. It was a large room with one king-size bed. He said the three of us would be sleeping in one bed, because the rest of the house was under construction.

He went on to say, "He lost his job and things were tough for him. The broken car caused him to be in a bind." I asked why he never shared this with me before I left America. He said, "He felt bad that a lot of preparation on my part had already been done and I already had a plane ticket and a VISA."

I was tired, irritable, and asked to wash up and lay down. The bathroom was semi modern with a shower stall, toilet, and pedestal sink, but there was no running water. There was a 25-gallon barrel of water with a bucket to be used for both bathing and cleaning up. I wished I had known those details before going there. It was like living in a run-down country. I'd never had that kind of experience.

When it was time for dinner, the kitchen was outside with a makeshift tin roof atop a concrete slab, with stools, a couple of tables, and lamps. There was a wood fire grill and a lot of coolers for food storage. The food was good but spicy. As we later prepared to sleep, I told him I traveled with an air mattress to protect my aching back. I desired to sleep on the floor, next to him and his girlfriend. I slept well but was mentally uncomfortable with the arrangements.

The next morning, I asked to speak to him in private. I told him, "I will be turning 50 years old in a couple of days and I'm too old to have come halfway across the world to sleep on the floor, in a place with no running water." I asked to be taken to a hotel.

My friend was quick to anger, "I'm sorry, I have fallen on hard times, and I expected you to understand and stay with us." I understood his opinion, but I still asked to be taken to a modern hotel and, I needed to exchange some of my United States cash for their Naira.

I settled in at the Hilton Hotel. It was large, beautiful, and modern. Upon checking in, I asked the manager if he could exchange my American money so that I could shop. He agreed. My friend and his girlfriend escorted me to my room. He protested my decision to stay there initially, but later relented.

When they left the hotel, there was a knock at the door. It was the hotel manager. He told me, "When I exchanged your money, I observed your friend asking for funds. He counted the Naira to the U.S. dollar incorrectly; and took more money than you were supposed to give him."

He said he could tell that I did not know the exchange rate and wanted to be sure that I learned quickly. He asked that I be careful because Nigerian people tend to extort money from Americans.

He offered to have a private driver take me shopping if I desired. I thanked him for his consideration and agreed to let him know my shopping plans. I had been betrayed by a man I had known for nearly 30 years. I felt empty, alone, and afraid. I would be celebrating my birthday with all of this drama, so far away from home.

The next day I prayed and meditated about the situation and heard a voice say, "GO HOME." My expectations of a celebration were no more. I cried and was angry about the preparations and funds spent to come to Nigeria.

I understood man will fail you every time, but God always wants the best for me.

I asked my travel agent to find me a flight back to America as soon as possible. I assured her everything was okay, but I needed to return home quickly. I explained that some things were not as I expected.

Later my friend and his girlfriend visited. I told them how I knew I had been swindled out of money by him, a friend I thought I could trust. He started to cry, saying how hard it has been since he returned home. He lost his job and now has a baby on the way. He said, "You have money and I needed it." I told him all he needed to do was to communicate with me honestly.

I told him my plans to go home as soon as I could get a flight out. He raised his voice in anger, carrying on about all the preparations for me to get there, and accused me of being rude to decide to just up and leave? I made it clear to him that I no longer felt safe there, asked them both to leave, and told him not to bother to call me ever again. I celebrated alone in the hotel's restaurant. They were nice enough to give me a cake and sing happy birthday.

I received my new flight information; I could not get out for five more days. I took this time to relax, read, pray, meditate, and do some shopping. I still had two weeks left for vacation. I started looking for other places to go once I arrived back home.

I decided to draft and execute a will, after my trip to Nigeria. I thought, if something happened to me, I knew my ex-husband would take care of our son, but I needed to make it legal. I actually did a full estate plan: will, power of attorney and living will. I made JC the executer, because I had no doubt he had my best interest at heart, and would take care of our son, my only child.

Although we both had problems within our marriage that had gotten out of control, he was truly remorseful and loved me just as much as I loved him. We simply lost focus on the marriage and went our separate ways while still married.

I continued to work and manage my mother's care. Her mentation began to wane, and she started to become aggressive and angry. I sought a home visiting doctor, because she tried to walk out of the doctor's office the week before. As I approached her, she flailed her arms and became belligerent. I knew this was the turn for the worse.

The home visiting doctor was kind and thorough with his assessment of Mom. She appeared anxious as he assessed her but allowed it to continue. He asked if I was ready, willing, and able to continue her care at home, to which I replied yes.

I explained how Mom had my brother and me and that was the only time she had been in a hospital, some 50 years ago.

She worked as a nurse's aide in a mental institution for 34 years, before retiring. She loved healthy eating and exercising, walking an hour each day. She had high blood pressure, which was under control with medicines, but no other illnesses.

I, being a nurse, knew I could keep her in her home until the end. I had knowledge of getting any medical equipment she would need, and I would take responsibility for doing her blood work when the doctor ordered. I had mental and physical support from the nursing aides Mom had, and support from my ex-husband. Mom took a liking to her aide, who was able to get Mom to do things I could not. One day I was scolding her about taking off her pullup diapers, and as I asked her not to do this, she replied, "Yes Mother." I looked at her with love and recognized I was being a little hard on her.

Emotionally, I loved my mother so much, I felt putting her in a nursing home would break my heart. She did not deserve to finish her life like that. She knew she was in her own home, and I would see that to the end. I presented my brother with a legal document, a do not resuscitate (DNR) form and let him know she would never go to a hospital unless an emergency situation occurred.

CHAPTER 19

Crossroads

While decompressing from my Nigeria experience, my ex called to say our son had committed domestic violence against his girlfriend. He had been arrested by the campus police and taken to the county jail and had been scheduled to go before a judge. The following day he got another call from the school advising that because the girlfriend refused to press charges he could not be held, but the presiding judge ordered him to leave the state of Connecticut for a year. He said he would only have an arrest report and he ordered him to be released. The school said because of this ruling our son was being expelled and we would have to get him and his belongings as soon as possible.

Because of my job and caring for Mom, I was unable to go with my ex, so he went alone. I felt angered and dismayed that my son would do such a thing. I believed they both were doing drugs and perhaps that's why she refused to press charges. When we visited the year before, we noticed how disheveled he and his girlfriend were. We asked them if they were doing any drugs, and they both denied they. We had no proof.

I could only imagine how hurt and angry his father was. He went on to Connecticut to pick up our son. He tested our son for drugs as soon as they got home, and he tested positive for everything but cocaine.

He appeared agitated and afraid. He had no clue the gravity of what had happened. He said they were with a group of other students hanging out around his dorm. They were all smoking marijuana. He said he observed his girlfriend kiss another student on the mouth and he got angry. He approached her and pushed her to the ground. Some of the students shoved him away from her, while another student called campus police. He said they knew what she did was wrong and singled him out as violent. He called them racist.

I explained that he should never hit, or as he said push anyone, let alone a woman. I let him know if he caused any physical harm to her, he would be in jail and there would be nothing his parents could do. He agreed to stop the use of marijuana. I then asked him about what was next for him and if he knew what he wanted to do.

He picked up odd jobs and tried to pick up his life, but I could see it was hard for him. At 20 years of age, he was having trouble integrating back into society. He started drinking and smoking marijuana again. His father told me he had stolen money from a 5-gallon water bottle, and he was not happy with the disrespect. When our son turned 21, his father said he would have to leave his home and inquired about him living with me and my mother. I agreed. For about five years of his life, he was all over the place, some nights he would not come home. Most times he would not even show up for a job that a family member had given him. It was as though he had no zeal nor desire for life and operated as such. I took him in because, no matter what, he was still our son. I immediately set ground rules and realized although he was chronologically grown, mentally and emotionally, he was a teenager gone rogue.

I was able to get his old job at a relative's business back, but he only worked, at best, 20 hours per week. He had excuses about not feeling well such as sore throats, sinus infections and he even went to work one day and complained of chest pains. He was seen by the paramedics, and nothing was found. It was later discovered he had smoked too much marijuana. It was just another excuse to get out of work. He would leave home most days pretending to go to work but was hanging out with friends smoking weed.

I remembered asking him if he recalled the conversation we had when he was 14 years old and confessed, he had been smoking weed for a while and he liked it. I asked if he remembered what I said about the abuse of alcohol or any drug and how it could greatly impact his adult life. He said yes. I told him, well here is your life.

I later had a talk with his father who said he believed we were good parents and did what we thought was best for our son. I added, we never abused him, mentally nor verbally. So, in essence we did what we could.

I told our son again, "Your father and I love you. We are educated and forward-thinking people and know that as you age into adulthood, your priorities are not in order." His father and I agreed that we did not have the power to make our son grow up; we simply had to allow him to walk on his journey to correction, which could take the rest of his or our lives. I set the bar a little higher and said I would no longer tolerate him living under my household and not taking care of his financial health and if it got any worse, he would have to leave. The day came when I was fed up and asked our son to leave. His father sanctioned it, and we helped him find a bed in a rooming house. It was one of the saddest days of my life; because I was finally freeing him to his own horrible decisions, but I had no other choice.

He lived in this rooming house for a couple of months but suddenly stopped paying the rent and became homeless. His father called one day to say he would take him back in. He didn't want to see him homeless. How bittersweet. He feared someone would kill him.

However, he continued on a downward spiral, not working, bathing, or taking care of himself, and refusing medical/mental health counseling. His father offered rehabilitation, but he would not go. We both knew, as his parents, we would have to stick closely together and ride out the wave of disconnection we were witnessing in our son – even the revolving door between his father's house and my house. The storm came in 2012 while I was in Washington, DC at a conference. The game plan was for our son to join me in Maryland after the conference for a family reunion. I bought a round-trip ticket for him and arrived in Maryland on Friday with anticipation of him coming in on Saturday morning.

While having an early dinner that Friday, I received a call from my hairstylist. She said she was aware I was out of town but needed to speak with me. She shared that my son asked her to groom his hair before his trip and she gave him the cost and he agreed to payment. When she was finished, my son instead told her, "bill it to my mom and charge an extra $100, she can pay it."

My stylist was quite upset. She also let me know that the two bicycles I had recently purchased had been sold by my son while I was away. I thanked her for the information and let her know I would pay her when I got home.

I immediately called my ex-husband and asked him to enter the house to see if the bikes were there and indeed, they were not, and neither was our son. I instructed my ex-husband to put the double-sided key lock on the door, because our son had no key to it. I also instructed him not to take our son to the airport the next day.

I felt that if he came to my location, one of us would be dead or in jail. I was furious that my own child would wait until I left town for work and take advantage by stealing items from our home and then cajole my hairdresser into doing his hair under false pretenses.

The lack of decent human respect was gone, and I began to notice his disrespectful behavior toward everyone. His behavior was narcissistic, taking everyone that cared about him for granted. He seemed like a sociopath to me. I went back to my hotel and was quite angry. I was in shock at this level of behavior and thought for sure, if he stepped foot in that hotel in Maryland, I would kill him.

I felt so betrayed and bewildered and knew my son had to be experiencing some kind of mental illness. I also knew I needed help for myself, because this dysfunctional living had gone on too long. It bordered on greed and crime. I knew I needed some professional help. He called several times over the next 24 hours, but I refused to answer the phone.

When I returned home, I had a chance to speak with him. I wanted to know what frame of mind produces such destructive behavior.

He nonchalantly responded, "This is how I live. I negotiate services from people to get my needs met." That statement was as shocking as his behavior.

The next day I made an appointment with my son's psychiatrist. When I finally met with her, she said she could not discuss anything about him. I let her know I was there for myself. We talked about what had occurred since he left college, how he had been kicked out of school for domestic violence. I told her the cascade of things around how he came back home. How he was first living with his father and started acting out by stealing money and taking cars without permission. I then told her how he refused to hold down a job and wanted to use cannabis as the medication of choice for his ADHD symptoms. I let her know how he had lived between my mother's home with me and his father's home. We both saw no change in his behaviors, and in fact things had gotten worse.

After stealing my car in the middle of the night, he wrecked it. I had to take him out of my home again. I explained how this way of living had made me depressed, and his father and I were getting nowhere in our efforts to parent him. I needed help mentally and emotionally to not accept him back.

She asked what fears I had about allowing him to be on his own. I admitted that I did not want to see the day that the police would come to tell me he was found dead somewhere. I began to sob uncontrollably, saying, "this is my only child."

She asked what powers I possessed to stop him from hurting himself. After a few minutes of silence, I realized I had none. She said it was obvious I was allowing him to abuse me by giving in to his demands and advised that if I did not stop my behavior, he would never grow up. She also said I could very well be killing myself by allowing the stress to hurt my body.

I thought long and hard about the session, and never saw a need to go back. I was healed of the false ideas I had for trying to raise a grown person. If I really cared for him, I would let him be himself. And whatever would come from that, even if he decided to kill himself, his life was not mine.

I put him out of my house again and only allowed periodic visits. We grew apart over the next couple of years, but I always stayed in touch with his father, who always seemed to keep up with him. It was refreshing to know he was alright, but still doing the same things.

I got a call one early morning from his father. He said our son had been arrested and if he called me for bail, to please NOT do anything. At first, this call felt intimidating, but I soon realized reality dictated that I must allow him to be who he is, even while in jail. He was jailed for resisting arrest. I let him know I would comply.

He then asked, "Can I tell you something? Jenny, I love you, and I've always loved you. I'm sorry our marriage did not work out. This is your only child and I fully understand your maternal desire to take care of him, but he is a man, and your behaviors of help won't help him. Due to his mental illness, there is always a chance he may take his own life, but you should know we have been great parents, but the time has come to back off."

He said he has watched our son carefully and knows he swindles and takes advantage of me at every turn. He asked me to cease giving him money, food, paying phone bills or providing any kind of transportation, to allow him to be a man. I said I would comply.

CHAPTER 20

Alzheimer's Observed

The next year was the hardest yet. I worried about my mother's failing health. She became weaker and found it hard to walk. I asked the doctor for a home x-ray to see if she may have fallen. That test came back negative. Her brain was failing and negatively impacting her ability to walk. She became bed bound; and soon after she stopped talking.

I was concerned about how to manage the next step. The medical team recommended hospice. Just the word hospice horrified me because that meant the end was near.

He said hospice at home was the best situation because it would lessen the burden on myself and the nurse's aide. She would be assigned a hospice doctor who would visit more often, as well as an RN to check for bed sores and monitor vital signs. They would also supply diapers and disposable bed pads, which Medicare would cover.

Hospice services could continue for as long as she needed care. When the end would come, there would be no need for an autopsy. The Do Not Resuscitate (DNR) Form would be enough for her to go straight to the funeral home of my choice. I needed time to think it over. I had not made any funeral arrangements for my mom and felt overwhelmed and unprepared for the end.

I continued with her current situation, ordering a hospital bed and all of the other equipment needed, since she was no longer mobile. I kept a close eye on her skin condition in an attempt to keep the pressure ulcers away.

I mustered up the courage to go to a funeral home close to her home to make burial arrangements. That day I went, I drove into the parking lot and sat in my car. I cried for her. I had never performed this duty before. It was hard.

I wiped my tears and entered. A man greeted me at the door, "Good afternoon, ma'am, how can we help you?" His voice was in a low tone, and his words were soothing.

I explained my needs and he ushered me to his desk. He explained that all I needed was a pre-need document. This is a transactional document which states what Mom's needs would be at the time of death. I chose burial over cremation. What followed caused my legs to shake and my palms to sweat. I needed to pick out a coffin that was in my price range. I looked at a few before choosing a soft baby blue coffin.

I gave him Mom's current health status and shared that she would be going into hospice care at home soon. I wanted her buried in her home city of Tallahassee. He looked at flight costs and further advised I would have to make the arrangements with a local funeral home to receive her body and take her to the grave site. I chose to have a memorial service in their small chapel and my brother, and I would make the other burial arrangements. We have a cousin in Tallahassee who manages Clifford Hill Cemetery. It sits on 20 acres of land that my grandfather donated to the church for the cemetery. My grandparents are buried there as well as all of my mother's siblings. She was the last one of them living.

As we sorted through the process of the pre-need, I felt relieved that I had made these decisions. He typed up all of the pre-need items they were to perform and gave me a quote. He then informed me that in the event of her death, the only price change would be any additional cost of flying her body. At that time, payment would be due.

Over the next few weeks, I thought about my options. I spoke with the caregiver about increasing her hours to 12 hours a day. She presented me with a different proposal. She said she and her family would use one of their bedrooms for Mom to stay in so Mom would have her 24 hours a day and she could avoid the long daily drive back and forth. She had been with Mom for five years and they had grown close.

She agreed to do this for the money I was offering. With the help of my son and the caregiver's husband, we moved the necessary furniture, medical items, and clothing, to their house. Mom seemed quite content with the move. She had visited her house many times before, especially when she was more mobile.

I remember when the caregiver first started, she had a six-month-old baby girl and an eight-year-old son. I introduced Mom to her, and she said, "What a beautiful baby." The caregiver sat the baby on the bed next to Mom, and we watched her begin to play with her tiny hands. The baby smiled and giggled. We both smiled. I knew this brought joy to Mom and we would have a successful outcome. I asked that she come to work dressed in regular clothing, so Mom wouldn't feel she needed a nurse, since she has been independent all of her life.

When I reminisce about when I first moved back home, she said many times, "Why are you here? Go home to your husband."

I would always reply, "I live here now, and laugh." She was not used to anyone being there with her.

The proposed arrangement went well. Mom continued to decline in mental and physical function. Watching her deteriorate was like watching the flame of a candle wane, but not go out. I did not want her to suffer like this, but there was nothing I could do but make sure she was safe. It seemed odd not to have her at home and I often felt alone.

The caregiver and I arranged for me to visit Mom every Sunday. I would collect any receipts from the petty cash we set up for Mom's food or disposable items. I would pay the caregiver and replace the petty cash. I would hold her hand, rub her face, and kiss her often, always telling her, "I love you." She would look at me, and I sensed she knew who I was, but by this time, she no longer spoke. I wished she would come back and be my mom, best friend, confidant, drinking buddy, and road dog, again.

Finally, the day came when the doctor said it was time to add the home hospice services for Mom. He said her skin was breaking down on her heels and knees. He wanted to order nursing services through hospice to manage wound care. I agreed. Mom was too far away for me to manage this care and it was time for some help. The care giver told me that she needed to go home to her country to honor the third year passing of her mother. She said it was tradition. I called hospice care to coordinate Mom being brought back home by ambulance and to have her hospital bed delivered as well.

On the day Mom arrived, I felt joy that she would be in her own home again, for a couple of weeks. I hired a fill-in caregiver who would be with her 12 hours a day. Hospice care was also coordinated.

When the ambulance arrived, they brought Mom into the house and then into her room. She began to look all around, as though she knew where she was. Soon she let out a loud wailing cry. I burst into tears, responding to her wail, "Yes, you are home now."

She had not spoken in nearly two years.

Over the next two weeks Mom went in and out of deep sleep. During her second week home, she stopped eating and went into a deep comatose state. The caregiver reported that she thought Mom might not make it through the week.

Two nights later I slept in Mom's old bed, next to the hospital bed. I rubbed her head and held her hand. I said, "Mom, it's okay to go. 'You were a diva, and you wouldn't like what you see now. I'm okay."

Around midnight I went to sleep in my bed near the rear of the house. I was awakened a couple of hours later by my son's screams. He had come by unexpectedly to check on his grandmother. He was running through the house shouting "She's gone Mom! She's gone!"

I jumped from my bed and we both ran to her room. She was gone at 2:00 am. My son and I sat on her bed, staring at her lifeless body.

I screamed out, "You're free now Mom! Free."

I stood and kissed her forehead. The loss was gut wrenching. As a registered nurse I had witnessed people pass away, but this was different. I was astonished that she chose to go after I left her presence. She did not want me to witness her dying. I thank her for that.

I called the hospice nurse to pronounce her dead officially. My son was inconsolable. I then called the funeral home to collect her remains. I called several family members, all of whom were relieved that her suffering was over. It felt all too real.

The next day we gathered at the funeral home to make final arrangements. I called the local funeral home in Tallahassee to receive her body. I arranged for her to be brought to the grave site. There would be a short service before lowering her into the ground. I called her extended family and friends with the announcement of the services to be held in Tallahassee. My cousin helped me to make the obituary. My brother and I gathered Mom's remaining funds from the bank to pay all the final costs.

A date was set for the memorial service to be held at the funeral home in Miami and a repast at her home. My brother and I would fly out the next day for the burial in Tallahassee. Her Tallahassee family would meet us at the gravesite for a brief memorial the following day. It all seemed so final. I sobbed as they lowered her casket into the ground. *Goodbye, Mom; my best friend.*

CHAPTER 21

Back on the scene

I was still single and no longer a caregiver for Mom, who had passed away, after 12 years of going through Alzheimer disease. I cared for her 9 of those years. Although I chose to care for her 24 hours a day with nursing help in her own home, I knew this would be best for her and she deserved to spend her last days being loved in the total comfort of a home she so loved.

I decided to take more Better Living Classes at my church and stick to them until I could complete the master's program. I've attended this church since 1998 and although I've taken several classes over the years, I did not feel I had mastered them well enough to handle my life spiritually i.e. living based on the teachings of Jesus Christ.

I dove into the classes again and it took two years to finish them. Now I felt empowered to receive a master's certificate, but this time I felt assured enough to manage my emotional health and dealing with my son.

My ex had gotten divorced after 10 years of marriage to wife number three and our son was again living with his father.

I began wondering if I could attract a reputable mate again. I had no time during the years I took care of my mother. I wondered how it would feel to fall in love again. I began to question if I was a suitable mate. I was 53 years old and felt unsure of the new dating arena.

I got into online dating, juggling three different sites in my spare time, on the weekends, and before bed. I liked that it was impersonal, that I was simply sending text messages to the online site, which then sent a message to the person in question. It gave me time to look at multiple pictures and profiles.

If the person said little about themselves, I did not pursue them. If they had no profile picture, I didn't pursue them either. After many telephone calls with men - I saw no match for me, I finally met a guy online and fell in love again after many years. This guy and I really jelled on the first date. When we first made phone contact, we spoke for four hours and enjoyed the conversation so much we arranged to meet the next day. Our relationship got off to a quick start, we found we had a lot in common and were willing to attempt to make a success of our union.

One day I purchased a coffee table from a thrift store and the staff was able to get it into my car, but when I arrived home my boyfriend could not get it out of the car without some help. I explained that the only men I knew to help him, would be my ex-husband and my son. He said that would be fine. I made the phone call and explained the situation and off to work I went.

I was still at work by the time my ex was available to stop by. When I got home, my boyfriend let me know he had met my ex-husband and my son. He did share that he thought JC was a nice man. He even asked him to have a beer! Though he declined the offer. My boyfriend said he wished he could have a good relationship with his ex-wife, as I have with my former spouse.

I explained that in truth, my ex-husband and I got over the initial anger after about a year of splitting up, and because we had once professed to love one another, we could still love each other and not be married.

We also did not want our mentally unstable son to think we hated each other.

I continued both relationships in peace and harmony. Soon I began to realize that I needed to fix

Mom's aging home if I was going to keep it. After my divorce I dreamed of owning my own home again. I fantasized what it would look like and where I might want to live. I thought of taking out a fresh mortgage on Mom's house to upgrade her home with some much-needed work. It needed a roof, all the windows and doors needed changing, and both bathrooms would need a complete overhaul. It would have to be done for me to continue to live there.

I called my bank and asked them to consider giving me a mortgage. In no time they approved it and set a date for an appraisal. I was excited. I made a list of the order the work needed to be done and I visualized turning the home into something modern for me. Soon I received a call from the bank informing me that the house had a 900 square feet undocumented building added onto it. I inquired about my options. The bank manager informed me that I would have to hire a contractor to get county officials to grandfather in the illegally built area.

I called a few contractors and two came to give me estimates. They all said their starting fee would be $10,000 and there was no guarantee the county would oblige and that their fee was non-refundable. Talk about a kick in the gut. I took this issue into prayer, meditation, and journaling. After two months, I decided to chase my dream of single home ownership. I found a realtor, and we worked together for three months, after fine tuning the type of home I desired. On the first day of house hunting, the last house I saw that day was the one I bought.

I placed Mom's home up for sale and an investment company bought it. Shortly after moving into my new home with my boyfriend and two dogs, we were scheduled to go to a family reunion. We had no one to keep the dogs, and the place was in disarray with furniture and boxes. I called my ex-husband to ask if he could help out. He was retired and agreed to come by the next morning for the keys and instructions.

My boyfriend said, "I can't believe he would agree to help us out in this way." I reminded him that just because we were not married, did not mean we couldn't be friends. Friends help out friends.

Later that year, I gave a New Year's Eve party and invited my JC to come with his new girlfriend. Everything was fantastic. The next day my ex-husband called and said that his girlfriend let him know she observed him at the party, and thought for sure, we were still in love with one another. I can't say she was wrong, because when were in each other's presence, there was significant love and respect, as God has love for us all. We knew that we just did not get along as a married couple, but we wished to keep our strong co-parent, friendly relationship as is.

One Saturday I received a call from my ex-husband. I could hear dinging and bell sounds in the background. As he began to speak, I asked where he was. He said he was in the hospital. I asked if I could visit. He said yes and gave me his room number.

I told my boyfriend about the phone call and shared that I would be visiting the hospital to see him that day. He asked if he could come along, and of course I said yes. When we entered the room, I walked over to the bed and kissed him on the forehead. Then my boyfriend who was behind me, proceeded to shake his hand, offering a blessing and a prayer.

The hospital visit went well. My ex-husband's aorta had a bulging on it and his blood pressure was running dangerously high. I asked if I could help in any way and told him and the hospital staff that I was only a phone call away. He was able to go home from the hospital in good condition after a week's stay. I stayed in touch at least weekly and after about three months, I discovered he had a new girlfriend.

CHAPTER 22

Re-connecting as friends

I worked in a healthcare center as an RN. I noticed one day that my ex-husband was on the schedule to be seen by the doctor I work with. I knew that he was very fond of this doctor, having met her on a few occasions, while attending parties at my home. He asked me about her level of expertise. I had him google her. I watched the schedule from my office to see when he would arrive. After he arrived and was placed in a room, I knocked on the door and peeked in to say hello.

I entered, walked over to where he sat and gave him a kiss on the cheek. He was accompanied by a woman whom he introduced as his girlfriend. I reached out to give her a handshake as I introduced myself. I inquired as to how he was feeling, and he replied, better than he had been. I left the room when the doctor entered.

This all occurred a few days before Valentine's Day. My ex-husband came back to the healthcare center the next day with a vase full of roses. I escorted him to my office. I asked, "What are the roses for?"

He replied, "Because I will always love you no matter who we are with." He said he wanted me to leave the roses on my desk because he knew my boyfriend would be bringing roses when he arrived home.

I jokingly said, "WOW! This is a shock; because you never bought me roses when we were married."

He responded, "You said, 'don't buy me any flowers, give me the money.'"

I said, "You are correct. But this feels different now." I thanked him and gave him a big hug.

He whispered, "Jenny, I Love you."

A few days later my ex-husband called to say his new girlfriend wanted to meet me and my boyfriend, perhaps over dinner. She wanted to get to know us better. He also shared that he was having more negative outcomes with his health problems, and the doctor wanted to run more tests. He sounded weary as he told me it was possible that he may need a few stints placed in his heart. With all the health challenges he was facing, the dinner plans never happened.

I did not see him for about 6 months, but we spoke regularly to track our adult son. We continued with our separate, but friendly lives, with us being mindful to respect each other's privacy. There were a few occasions when I asked to be picked up from the airport, because I traveled quite a bit for work. My boyfriend worked the evening shift and was rarely available to get me at night.

There were a few occasions that my ex-husband brought his girlfriend along. One time in particular, I invited her into my home as my ex-husband was bringing in my luggage. She accepted and we sat around and had a glass of wine. She seemed nervous at first, but I did my best to make her feel comfortable. After all she was a guest in my home.

On another occasion when they picked me up from the airport, upon arriving home, my boyfriend was just arriving home as well. I introduced him to my ex-husband's girlfriend. My boyfriend seemed happy to see my ex-husband again. He said now we can have a beer together. The atmosphere was calm and peaceful.

CHAPTER 23

Boyfriend Drama

It was the morning of Mother's Day 2017. I invited a church member to join us for dinner. I visualized the occasion as quiet and peaceful. My boyfriend asked if he could invite his coworker over to join us. He worked one Sunday a month and would be working prior to the start of the dinner. I asked him to hurry home after work to grill the shrimp and fish. He agreed.

I was aware of this coworker, as he had spoken about her before. He worked as a supervisor of janitorial services at the public school system. He had always spoken of his relationship with many of his co-workers. This time though it felt odd. I never knew him to socialize with them and out-of-the-blue he was asking to invite a female coworker to our home.

I asked, "Why would she not want to spend time with her family?"

He replied, "Her family no longer lives local, and she is alone."

My spidey senses were on high alert, yet I decided to simply be kind and said, "Sure she can come over."

I had encountered her before. My boyfriend asked if I would meet him one Friday night at a local tavern for chicken wings and beer, he said a coworker I did not know of would join us. I thought nothing of it and met them as planned

I sat alongside him in the booth and she across the table. I found her to be an ordinary looking woman with a big smile. She gazed at him often and giggled like a child at all his jokes. It was uncanny how she behaved. He and I didn't talk about her again until this moment.

My church member came a little early to assist me with preparing the Mother's Day meal. Not long after I went into the bedroom to freshen up while she stuffed, garnished, and plated the deviled eggs. I heard my boyfriend's voice speaking to someone else in the house. I knew the voice of my friend, and it wasn't her.

I yelled out, "John, is that you?"

He replied yes.

I asked, "Who are you talking to?"

He replied, "I'll be right there."

As I continued to freshen up, he appeared in the bedroom.

I asked, "Who were you talking to?"

He replied, "It's my coworker. I was trying to show her to the family room, so she could watch the football game. I also needed to show her how to use the remote control and get her a drink."

I said, "Wow. You actually came into this house for the first time and did not say, *'Honey I'm home.'* Did you bring your coworker here?"

He replied, "Yes, no need for her to drive."

A cold feeling came over me and I thought *this is not going to turn out good*. Something was going on. He went outside to grill the seafood. I emerged from the bedroom to see my friend looking perplexed.

I said to her, "I'm perplexed too."

I entered the family room to re-introduce myself. She stood to shake my hand, saying "Thanks for letting me come over. I found myself alone this Mother's Day because my children have moved away."

I took a deep breath and remarked, "You are welcome. I hope you enjoy yourself." As my boyfriend started the shrimp kabobs, I noticed him rush inside to share those with his coworker. The vibe was bad from the time he came into my home with her. His behavior was blatantly disrespectful.

When it was time to serve dinner, the two of them went off to eat in the family room. My church member and I chose the dining room. As dinner finished, I asked my boyfriend to have a word with him. He said yes and we proceeded to the bedroom.

I shared, "This has been an odd, eerie type of evening and I am calling it quits. Please take your coworker home now."

When he returned home, he discovered I had asked my church member to leave before he got back. I asked him to join me in the family and have a seat. He looked nervous.

I asked, "Do you have some type of relationship with your coworker, other than work?"

He replied, "Don't be facetious. I'm her supervisor and I don't fraternize with my employees."

I shot back, "Well, let me paint a picture of what I observed."

I took a deep breath and released everything, "You and I have lived here for the last three years. There has not been one time that you have come home and not made your presence known. You stopped by this person's house to pick her up as though she was your date. You bring her here and parade her in front of our TV, refuse to come when I called you, until you could instruct her on our remote control and lastly get her a drink, you then proceed to cook the seafood, but came in a few times to give her an early taste of our shrimp. I deduce that you like this woman, and before you speak, I want you to know that it is alright with me. People fall in and out of love all the time. Please find a way to come clean about this and let's discuss our options."

He looked deflated and said he was going to bed because he had a long day. We never discussed that coworker again.

In 2017, after five years of dating my boyfriend, I went to South Africa for my 60th birthday, with a coworker. My boyfriend had no desire to go and agreed to stay behind and keep the dogs and the house. A hurricane warning forced me to fly out early to New York, 5 days ahead of the trip. I took shelter in a hotel in Queens while waiting for my travel date.

The morning that I was leaving New York for Africa, I received a phone call from my boyfriend. He said, "Hello I know you are on your way to the airport, but I need to tell you something, so you don't have to hear it from the neighbors." He said that the neighbors might notify me that I had some woman in the house.

I asked what in the world he was speaking of. He spun a story about the woman being a coworker who had lost power in her home during the hurricane. And while our home also had no power, he invited her to come over because my home had a generator.

In those few short moments, I realized I had a big decision to make. Do I blow up on the phone and threaten his life? Or do I ask God for peace and continue with my 10 thousand dollars, three-week trip to Africa? I chose the latter and simply said, "Please be mindful of doing anything in my home with your coworker that is out of order. If you choose differently, I will know it when I return home."

I was visibly shaken and wondered what I did in the relationship to be disrespected in that way. He was someone I respected and loved for five years. There was nothing I could do, so I carried on. When I returned from the trip, I was again picked up by my ex and his girlfriend and I invited them in for a glass of wine, which I surely needed. While we were discussing the highlights of my trip, my boyfriend came home from work with flowers. He greeted my ex, and his girlfriend gingerly and then kissed me on the cheek.

My ex soon left, and I pretended my boyfriend was not there. I proceeded to undress and put away my toiletries. He was also quiet. Moments later, he stepped into the master bedroom and said he was tired, and he had a long day coming up.

I said "Goodnight."

He responded, "I'll be sleeping in the guest room."

Over the next few weeks, I refused to have the coworker conversation, so I could sense an uneasiness in him. I saw no reason to open an old wound, causing me distress. He was quiet, cold, and distant in his interactions with me. My intuition let me know, he was wearing all of his guilt, and I was not allowing him to discuss it.

More weeks went by, and I had been making gestures about having sex, which he refused. There it was. Our relationship was taking a turn for the worse. We continued on this path past the Christmas and New Year holidays and still no loving emotions were shown by him. One Sunday morning I asked if he would grill some fish for me later in the day. He had to work a half day. He returned home to cook the fish. After he finished, he said he would be going bowling and not to expect him until after midnight.

I thought that was quite odd, because it was only five p.m., and he didn't ask me to go bowling with him. That bothered me and as I wondered what was really going on, I googled bowling alleys near my home. I found one less than five miles away.

I got my keys and took a ride to the location. As I entered the parking lot, I perused each row of cars looking for his car. There it was. I parked a couple of rows away and went into the bowling alley. I took a seat at the bar, which was near the front door.

I ordered a glass of wine and carefully looked at each lane to see where he was. I spotted him about nine rows down, bowling with his coworker, the same woman he had invited into my home during the hurricane and for Mothers' Day. A sick feeling rose in my stomach.

I sat and watched them interact with one another and although they were bowling, they looked like lovers. Not long after I arrived, I saw my boyfriend head toward the bar. I felt a need to get out of there, but he was coming toward the bar really quickly. He stood at the bar beckoning the server, and then he ordered a drink. While he was waiting, he saw me and walked toward me. When he got near, he reached for me, and I moved away and asked him not to touch me. I could tell he knew I was upset. He turned and walked away without his drink.

I thought it would be best if I left the bowling alley. My emotions were too high, and I knew this level of anger was not good for my blood pressure. I drove straight home.

When he arrived home way after midnight, I attempted to calmly talk about the situation. He said he had done nothing wrong, and he simply felt he was more compatible with the coworker than he was with me.

This statement blew my socks off because I could see that as his truth. I abruptly walked away and went to the bedroom and locked the door. All night I tossed and turned about my future with him and all I could see was taking any opportunity I could to settle this situation quickly and fairly. I needed to rid myself of him, his actions and behavior hurt deeply me.

The next morning, Monday at 6 am, I found him asleep in the guest room. I woke him up and said, "You have to leave my home this week. I will give you until the end of the week to pack and go. In the interim, I will be leaving to give you the space you may need." Two days later, I flew to Mississippi until the beginning of the following week.

During the plane ride I thought of how cunning and dishonest my boyfriend was. He was a coward and a cheat. He obviously had lost all respect for me and wasn't man enough to simply bow out of our relationship. I felt sad at the thought of being alone again. Another failed relationship.

I began to cry and then sob as the flight attendant asked, "Ma'am, are you alright?" The seat next to me was empty, so she sat down and asked me why I was crying.

I answered, "I asked my boyfriend to leave my home for his infidelities after five years of what I thought was a good relationship. We had traveled on more than 26 vacations to various places by cruises and road trips. I am angry and hurt." She offered me a glass of wine as I looked out the window at a beautiful sunrise.

Upon my return, he had left many personal items that he obviously no longer needed. I grabbed garbage bags and loaded them up with everything he left. The anger was still boiling within me. I thought of his cowardly behavior for choosing to be in a relationship with someone else and think he could string me along as well. I called that arrogance and blatant disrespect. I had given him the opportunity to walk away many months before. I thought he must have hated me; I knew he wasn't fond of my direct behaviors or the orderly process in which I lived. I tried on numerous occasions to get him to talk about any difficult areas in his life, but his machoism wouldn't allow him to speak.

I tried to disguise my pain by taking on more work and traveling to avoid the loneliness. I began drinking more than usual and I couldn't sleep without a bottle of wine a night. I started going to the casino on weekends, where I found the loneliness less painful. Although I knew no one there, I could interact with other patrons at the blackjack table. A few of my friends noticed my drinking and expressed concern.

I decided to Uber to and from events, knowing I would be drinking and to avoid a possible driving under the influence charge. One night I fell asleep in an Uber. When we arrived at my home, the driver had to wake me up. I was startled, but I gathered my belongings and got out of the car. I lost my balance and fell to the ground.

I heard the driver screamed, "Oh my God!" as he rushed out of the car to assist me.

I told him I would get up on my own. I turned onto my hands and knees and attempted to stand, but my left leg went out from under me, and I fell to the ground again. Being a nurse, I knew something was broken. I asked the driver to go up to the door and ring the bell, which he did. I had a house guest in from California at the time. When my friend opened the door, she started yelling when she saw me on the ground. She bolted from the house, crying "What's going on? Are you, okay?"

I asked her to call 911. As she retrieved my cell phone and made the call, I told her that I had fallen after stepping from the car. I laid there on the ground and rolled slowly onto my back looking up at the dark sky sobbing. I thought, *Okay, now I've hurt myself because of him.*

We both assured the Uber driver he could leave, which he did hesitantly. My friend said she would call my ex-husband who was my emergency contact, and she followed the ambulance to the hospital where I was able to get the emergency help I needed. It turned out that I had broken my left hip.

My friend explained to my ex what had occurred, and he told her to let me know, he would travel down to care for me by the time the surgery was completed. On the day I was to be discharged, he came diligently to the hospital awaiting instructions. He said he had been to my home and attempted to move furnishings around to accommodate me using a walker. As always, I felt so safe and secure with this person, whom I knew loved me.

The nurse wheeled me to the car, and it took 10 minutes for the three of us to figure out how I would get my affected leg inside. That was a laugh out loud moment. Once we arrived at my home, we both struggled to get me out of the car and into the house. Once inside, we now needed to decide where I would sit. At this point I was simply worn out and in pain. It had been a long day.

We chose the two-seater recliner in the family room. There we sat for a while plotting how to care for me. After about an hour, I decided to go to my bedroom and lie down. He put the walker in front of me and as I attempted to grab hold of it, my hip hurt so bad I went back down into the recliner.

He then said," I'll stand in front of you and help pull you up."

We were unsuccessful with that idea as well. I asked him to sit down so we could develop another strategy. We both burst out laughing, which drew laughing tears. What a shit show. Finally, I decided to get a better grip on the arms of the recliner before attempting to stand. From there I was able to then grab the walker to a full stance. We were still in tears laughing. Two educated people who knew nothing about physical therapy, including me, the registered nurse.

He and my son would alternate duties. He would be with me during the day and our son would stay at night. One day while JC was caring for me, I asked him for the first time, in 18 years, if he would accompany me to our annual Christmas party. He agreed. We both wore white, and I decorated my walker with Christmas lights. My co-workers took many pictures, and the CEO of the company called me a tough bird for making any attempt to attend the party in my condition. I remarked that I had not missed a company party in 18 years and wasn't about to miss this one.

I introduced him to my ex-husband, and he remarked, "I've never seen you before. Where have you been?" We all laughed. The physician I worked for, who was also my ex-husband's doctor, took lovely pictures of us. I was thankful to her but didn't realize just how grateful I would be later on.

CHAPTER 24

Everything Must Change

The respect my ex-husband and I had for one another during our breakup, was what I needed to practice for my peace of mind. I knew 3 months before that the relationship with my boyfriend was over, but I was hoping against hope. I took the opportunity to tell my ex-husband about the breakup.

I was still feeling let down and betrayed. We sat outside as I told him all the sorted details. He listened carefully and asked no questions.

Finally, when I was finished, he explained, "Men, most times do dumb things, and it's not that they don't love their mates, it's that they get caught up in competition and stupidity, trying to show off before women. It's often sexual and nothing more."

He went on to say that he believed my boyfriend was a decent and kind man, but allowed his ego to act for him, which led to destruction. He said he knew I was hurt, but that I was strong, and I would bounce back, and he would help anyway he could.

The conversation was comforting as he had been a comfort in many ways since our divorce. I knew he still loved me, and I felt the same. I always told myself the truth. Here is a man I fell in love with, all those years ago, that I truly respected, but I could not and did not want to be married to anymore. I kept that separation in my mind at all times. On a few occasions, he would call me just to say he loved me. I would let him know I felt the same.

One time he asked, "Since we get along so well now and have been for a few years, why couldn't we be remarried?" I explained that I was happier with our post-divorce relationship than our actual marriage. I grew up and became more responsible with my life as a result of being married to him.

We both had been in other relationships, and he remarried and divorced again. We'd managed all of that successfully and remained kind to one another. I told him I had taken the time to recognize what type of love and relationship we would be able to have with one another, and a married one was not for me. If we were to re-marry, I feel we would run the risk of damaging the real love we have for one another, which is Gods unconditional love.

We drew closer together over the next few months, as I healed from my emotional and physical injuries. As he was enjoying retirement and I was single again, we spent more time together, even though he still had a girlfriend. He spoke to me one day about his personal business, about the home we used to own together. Although I no longer had any ownership in the home, it seems he was compelled to tell me his current situation.

He stated that he needed a new place to live, because the home was being taken by the county because of imminent domain. An extension to the highway nearby would claim homes and businesses in that area. He said he was trying to buy another home, but his credit was not good enough for a new mortgage. He had his retirement money but let me know he would have to rent a place for the short term to qualify for a home.

After he left, I thought long and hard about him having to pay rent at his age. I thought of how I learned a lot about paying bills and saving money from him. He would always say, "Try to own your own home no matter what you may have to do to get it done." I began thinking about possible ways of assisting him.

After all we had been through over the years as a divorced couple, I felt that he would do anything for me, and I could perhaps extend the same grace. I thought perhaps I could help him out with my great credit score along with the large amount of money he had in his retirement account. The next day I called my credit union to inquire if I could qualify for a second home loan. The gentleman asked several; questions, and I noted to him that I wanted to purchase a second home for my ex-husband.

He jokingly replied, "Wow! Can you buy me a home?" Of course, we both laughed.

He asked permission to run my credit and look at my income and said yes. He said I could qualify for a second home up to $200 thousand dollars. The home would have to be 50 miles from my current home in order to be considered a second home. I thanked him and promised to get back to him.

When I saw my ex again, I let him know what I had done. I said I wanted to assist him in the purchase of a new home for himself, with my good credit and his cash. He looked at me in awe and began to cry. I felt saddened to see him cry and said, "Wow, in 37 years of knowing you, I have only seen you cry the day your mother passed away and the day our son was born."

He said, "I had to learn how to cry after the birth of my daughter with disabilities. She will never be like other children and will require 24-hour care to survive."

I told him that I could only imagine how hard it has been for him and the child's mother to now co-parent. He said co-parenting was never an issue, but the toll the caregiving has taken had become hard. His daughter was 15 years old and lifting her had been increasingly harder.

I told him to go 50 miles from my home address and find himself a house. He continued looking at me with tears in his eyes. I felt his pain and his joy at my offer to buy him a home.

With the cost and distance restraint placed on me purchasing another house, my ex and his girlfriend looked for a home within the given price range in other parts of Florida. The ones in the two surrounding counties were way over budget. Soon the girlfriend found a charming home 165 miles away in a sleepy town called Winter Haven. I quickly got to work, providing the bank and the real estate company with the many documents needed.

I was soon informed that since I was buying the home for my ex-husband, that his name would not appear on the deed, unless I put up all of the cash including the down payment and closing cost. He could not use any of his money toward the purchase. We put our minds together and decided I would transfer 50-thousand dollars from my 401K to my savings account. After the down payment and final sale was complete, he would reimburse me by certified check, and I would send the funds back to my 401k to avoid having to pay taxes.

We closed the deal on the last day of May 2018. It was joyous for both of us, he got a new home, and I was preparing to go on my first singles' cruise, since ending the relationship with my boyfriend. We celebrated over a steak dinner with his girlfriend.

She was curious as to why I would purchase a home for my ex-husband. I knew she would not understand what I was about to say, but I said it anyway.

"We were madly in love when we first met, and after many years of a successful marriage, we started to go our separate ways in our minds. I found myself wanting my single life back. Although he was okay with the status quo of us not acting like a married couple anymore, he agreed to allow me my freedom. He said he wanted to hold me to the marriage until our son graduated high school, but he saw a need for me to set my soul free. He said, if it meant me leaving, then do so."

I let the girlfriend know that the professionalism that we espoused could not break the bond of our 38-year relationship. "When he announced he would not be able to purchase a home after retirement, because of his poor credit score, my thoughts were, I can help with that.

I could lend him my good credit, because I know he has a significant amount of retirement funds to afford a purchase."

I told her he would more than likely do the same for me.

"My love for my ex-husband is not romantic anymore, but it has always been as God's love is, which would never go away. I would always be more than willing to help him in any difficult situation."

He and his girlfriend moved and settled into their Winter Haven home quickly with both of them commuting back and forth for personal and medical business.

Shortly after, my son and I were able to visit. The home was situated in a retirement community in a secluded cul-de-sac that was quiet and close to a huge lake.

My ex-husband called me the next month, highly upset that the bank was not honoring his direct payments for the mortgage. He was caring for his handicap daughter in his new home. Her mother was in Miami, and it was the first time the daughter had been away from her.

I asked him to calm down, reminding him that his explosive behavior was not good for his health. I reminded him that he was alone there caring for his daughter and if he were to have any type of medical distress, his daughter would not be able to call 911.

I painfully thought no one would know the situation occurring there and they were 166 miles away from all family and friends. I agreed to call the bank and straighten out the issue. I also placed a call to his only relative, other than his children. I let her know the situation. We spoke about how volatile he could be when angry, which was not good for his health. She agreed to call him multiple times a day.

CHAPTER 25

The End of an Era

On December 18, 2018, JC came back for the next step in a series of dental procedures to complete implants. He stopped by to check on me, since I was still in physical therapy two days a week, and still using a walker. We settled down in the family room to chat.

Later I had gone out to the garage for some beverages when he burst through the door. He was holding his chest and crying for me to call 911. My neighbor, who was a paramedic saw the commotion and rushed over. We got JC to sit down, while I spoke to the 911 operator and my neighbor was taking his vital signs. I was trying to comfort him, but it was obvious that he was in a lot of pain. He looked like he was in grave distress. It seemed like it took forever for the paramedics to come.

They quickly whisked him away and told me to follow them in my car. I was terrified driving to the hospital; I didn't know if he had passed away in the ambulance. I wondered what he must be thinking. I felt so sad. He was alone and in pain.

When I arrived at the emergency room, he was still on the paramedic stretcher, and he was vomiting green bile. The paramedic reported that he began to vomit during transport. He continued to moan and scream at times in pain. After a few minutes he was placed in a in one of the emergency room cubicles. The nurses were giving him more pain medicine, one of which was fentanyl, a very potent drug. Although I had recently broken my hip and couldn't walk nor stand without a walker, I managed to stand over him attempting to comfort him as best I could.

After glancing at the cardiac monitor, I noticed the EKG rhythm was normal with a small amount of rapid intermittent heart rate. He continued to vomit small amounts of bile and it dawned on me as an RN for many years, that his problem had to come from either his liver, gall bladder or pancreas. This was not a heart issue.

JC had been admitted to the hospital 5 years prior with a bulging of his aorta. His blood pressure always ran exceedingly high which caused this problem. He was kept in the hospital to decrease this risk of an abdominal aneurysm. He remained there for a week. He was discharged on several medicines and told to monitor his blood pressure daily.

After remembering this prior issue, I swiftly made my way to the nurses' station, where I asked to speak to the attending doctor. I told him about his prior aortic problem and asked could he order a sonogram of his gastrointestinal tract. I went back to be with my ex who had nearly turned himself over in the gurney as he writhed in pain. He looked at me and said, "Jenny I feel like I'm dying."

I responded, "Please don't say that."

Soon the sonogram technician entered the cubicle to administer the test. He took one look as the scan printed a page, tore it off and ran out of the cubicle, leaving the machine. I said to myself *"This does not look good."*

Shortly after, the doctor ran in and informed us that his aorta had ruptured, and they needed to do a CAT scan to determine the amount of rupturing. My ex said to the doctor "My kidneys are not able to accept the dye, my kidneys could shut down."

The doctor replied, "If we don't do the CAT scan now, you are going to die today anyway."

He asked JC if I could sign for the procedure, and he nodded yes. The nurse started a second IV line for the administration of the dye and they whisked him to the CAT scan room.

I was left outside the open door, with a clipboard to sign for the procedure. No less than a few minutes later, I heard a blood curdling scream from JC. I knew he had passed away. I melted down to the floor within my walker and began to chant, "Not my will, but God's will be done for JC's life."

They whisked JC into another room where they attempted to bring him back, but I knew they would not be able to do anything for him.

The devastation within me was horrific as I was taken up from the floor just as the doctor said, "Let's call the time of death, 5:18 pm, December 18th, 2018." He had only been retired for 15 months and was enjoying his new home.

As I sat outside of the curtained room, listening to them attempt to bring him back, I sobbed uncontrollably. The doctor came out to tell me he was gone, and they did all they could do. He asked if I wanted to go inside and be with him.

I stated, "I've stood over him for the last four hours, watching him die, and I will not see him dead. That would haunt me for the rest of my life."

I knew through my grief, that I needed to gain control and make decisions now for JC's remains. I did not want his body to remain in the hospital. He died a man divorced three times, but I knew deep within he would do the same for me.

The post-divorce relationship JC and I had, was ride or die. Our bond was tighter in his death than ever before during our 38-year relationship. I called a local community funeral home and asked the owner to send someone to pick up his body and that I would not leave the hospital until it was done. In that action, my grief was palpable.

I remained steadfast in my duties with great difficulty. I notified his four sons and the one remaining cousin that he had. I asked his eldest son to notify his mother, who was wife number one, and lastly, I notified his third wife and current girlfriend. I notified my son and stepson to come to the hospital as soon as they could, that their father had passed away.

His body and I were still in the emergency department when my son arrived. He hugged and kissed me on the forehead. He said, "Dad is now at peace."

He walked behind the curtain and said nothing. I could see his legs circling the gurney. I began thinking about all the people who would be impacted by JC's death.

He and his third wife co-parented their child with special needs. Trying to care for her without her father would be a huge impact. I thought of our son who had his mental health challenges. He relied heavily on his father for housing, mental and emotional support, as well as financial support. His oldest son, who had six children, loved their grandfather, especially when they received money unexpectantly.

His two sons from his girlfriend would also feel the impact. The oldest son of the two had not had a great relationship with his father until after their mother died. JC reached out to try and salvage their relationship. He would speak of how this son was attending school to be a chiropractor and how proud he was of him. JC showed me pictures of him, and he heavily resembled his father and looked like a model.

His third son, who we brought to our home and took care of him until he graduated from high school, kept in touch. He called his father less than a year before he died, to come be with him after he lost his wife, who was his high school sweetheart. She succumbed to a blood clot in her lung. They were both in their late thirties at the time. He rushed to be by his side. JC worried about the mental and emotional impact this had on his son, and how there was nothing he could do.

JC carried a ton of burden for the negative occurrences in his life. He spoke often of how he wished his little girl, his fifth and last child, could walk and be normal. He was sad all the time about her condition but wore it well. His stories told it all.

He said on many occasions how he still loved me and was sorry he ran me away. I believe he didn't see a way out of his misery. Two weeks before he died, we sat out on my veranda and he said, "Jenny I'm tired. I don't want to run around seeing the myriads of doctors and taking tests my primary doctor has ordered. I'm tired." I did not understand that he was giving up his life with these words. I didn't know how sick he had gotten.

The funeral home arrived to retrieve his body, but my stepson had not arrived. I asked if he could come back in an hour. He kindly said yes. My son exited and asked me to go home, he would sit with dad and wait on his brother. I gave him the funeral home's number to call when the two of them were ready.

I felt blessed that JC and I had sense enough to let go of our differences and be the best support for each other and our son.

I spoke to JC's eldest son about burial arrangements. I realized that he may not have had the funds, because he and his wife were raising six young children. I offered to pay for everything, and he agreed.

Later that day, I was scheduled to attend my first session of physical therapy. I was still shaken and sad, and I pondered not going. As I sat still with my thoughts, I heard JC say, "Come on baby girl, get up and go to therapy, that's the only way you will heal your hip."

I began sobbing again. I did as I heard, got dressed, and off I went. When I arrived, the receptionist said, "Where is your husband, I mean ex-husband?"

I replied, "He died yesterday."

She looked at me in horror and said, "He was just here with you on Friday. What happened?"

I began to cry and said, "He had a heart attack." I was in no way going to explain how he really died. I didn't have it in me. I did good just to get here.

The next few days were filled with funeral preparations and extended notifications to his children, other family members, ex-wives, current girlfriend, friends, and co-workers. My stepson drove down from a neighboring county to console my son and me. He was instrumental in gathering the names of all of his nieces and nephews. This was the son I partially raised.

I later received a call from the funeral director, that his eldest son called to say he would be handling all of the arrangements himself, even though he lived in another state. I let the funeral director know that was fine with me. I explained, I was nursing a broken hip and attending physical therapy every other day.

I said JC is his father, and I was only trying to help. I notified his only living sibling about the new changes. She said she had visited him and his wife recently and knew they had no way to pay for a funeral. She agreed to call him. A couple of hours later, the funeral home director called again, saying he had spoken at length with the son and asked for a credit card as a deposit until he could decide what to do. He said the clock was ticking, because he would have to get permission to embalm JC as soon as possible.

He said the son stated he really did not have all of the money for the burial, nor a credit card for the cost discussed. He said the son had agreed to allow me to move forward with whatever I decided. Here it was, back on my plate. The gravity was beginning to take a toll on me. I cried often and was unable to sleep. I had to make an awful decision on a funeral date.

JC passed away on the 18th of December, seven days before Christmas. Surely, I would not attempt to get everything in order that quickly. I vacillated with this for days. I decided on the 29th, a Saturday just before the New Year. I paced myself and took time from work to put this event in order. I called on JC's cousin to get me all of the family's names which should appear on the obituary as well as any other information I might need.

I asked my son and cousins to help me put a program in order. My son was saddened by his father's death. I explained that he should feel blessed because he had his father's presence his whole life. The other sons only had him partially in their lives. I needed his help to do right by his father. He agreed.

I got my cousin who is an elder in his church to give me an obituary format, he had done so when my mother died. I used a local printing company that I use for work. The owner agreed to do the printing for free. Lastly, I asked his third wife to sing a song, because I remembered JC loved her singing. She didn't think she could do it, but I managed to convince her. In fact, I shared it would be a travesty for someone else to sing.

We struggled to find the most recent photo of JC; then I remembered the doctor I work with had taken photos of us at the company's Christmas party. I reached out for her to send them to me.

JC looked like the 28-year-old I had met all those years ago when he passed. How could that be? The photo was taken on December 8th, and he was gone by December 18th. My heart was even sadder.

We finally got all of this information to the printing company. While at the printers, my son asked if a picture of a boat anchor could be placed behind his father's face? He said his father was the anchor for many people. I thought how poignant and true that was.

JC always remained in contact with every one of his family and friends. His connection to them seemed unbreakable. His direct family and extended family such as my mother, his two other mothers-in-law, all five of his children as well as grandchildren. He was kind, knowledgeable, and generous. He and I laughed a lot about people and the situations they find themselves in. He would say, "They don't see their choices." I came to know what he meant. We all have choices, but we don't see them, so the choice we don't make is still a choice.

The Friday before the service was set for the wake, I explained to the funeral director that I would not be in attendance. I had a physical therapy session that day and frankly I was exhausted. My son and JC's cousin would be there to officiate and meet the guests. The only request I had was for the coffin to be opened a couple of hours before the service and closed promptly at the start of the service. I watched Clarence start the dying process in my home and watched him pass away. To see him in a coffin was not a memory I wished to have.

The morning of the service, my home was full of relatives and friends. Although everyone was trying to get dressed and yelling at the young people, things seemed to go well. As we arrived at the funeral home, I was greeted by a few of his co-workers, his first wife, eldest son, and his wife, the second and third son, his third wife and their beautiful daughter.

JC remarked once, he was so happy to have finally had a daughter after 4 sons. But was angry and heartbroken that her disabilities would keep her from ever being a normal child.

The service got started and my family officiated the obituary. I had one of JC's co-workers say a few words about him and followed with the four boys saying a few words about their father. The eulogy was given by JC's most trusted friend from the age of 17. They were thick as thieves, he used to say. And finally, his third wife sang a beautiful song acapella. As she began finishing the song, she started to weep, her voice began to crack and she seemed to lose her balance as she left the podium, still singing.

People were standing and clapping as well as crying. His first wife, who sat directly behind me got up and went to assist the singer and even though I was nursing a broken hip, I stood to join them. I softly said to the crowd, "Here lies a man that has three wives at his funeral. Even in death he was well loved, and no one was at odds with each other. He set a beautiful precedence for us all."

Everyone stood and clapped again. I want to believe they were clapping for him. He deserved the honor. JC played a vital role in my life as I grew up from the age of 23, when I met him. I learned true love, forgiveness, compassion, joy, laughter, stillness, and peace.

www.ingramcontent.com/pod-product-compliance
Ingram Content Group UK Ltd.
Pitfield, Milton Keynes, MK11 3LW, UK
UKHW021258180426
11947UKWH00015B/903